# ROOM FOR GOD?

# ROOM FOR GOD?

## A Worship Challenge for a Church-Growth and Marketing Era

## ROBERT WENZ

*Foreword by* Michael Horton

*Renewing*
*Total Worship*
Ministries

© 1994 by Robert Wenz
Renewing Total Worship Ministries
9946 Red Sage Drive
Colorado Springs, CO 80930

Printed in the United States of America

**Library of Congress Cataloging-in-Publication Data**

**Wenz, Robert –**
 Room for God? / Robert Wenz, foreword by Michael Scott Horton

 Includes bibliographical references.
 ISBN 1-4196-7562-1

 1.   Worship. 2.  Public Worship. 3. Evangelicalism. I. Title
 BV10.2.W36  1994
 264-dc20                                        93-32051

# DEDICATION

While every book on worship is rightly dedicated to our
great God
who alone is worthy of worship,
it is also dedicated to all those
who are standing firm for the truth of God's Word
in a challenging era.

# CONTENTS

# FOREWORD

"The ultimate question is simple enough: Is there room for God in our worship?" The author of this insightful volume takes us to the heart of this matter of worship. Robert Wenz knows the marketing world: its subtle seductions, positive insights, and popular lingo. That makes for an interesting, well-informed, and balanced analysis that eschews either a naive rejection of all attempts to attract the unchurched or an uncritical acceptance of the Church-of-What's-Happening-Now.

We lament the fact that public education has been reduced to relativism and subjectivism (the study of math being replaced with the student's feeling about math), but we seem less concerned—or perhaps less aware—of the same influences in our own churches. Doctrine is replaced with "feel-good" or "do-good" sermons; a God-ward focus is replaced with human-ward and even self-centered orientation. We seem to believe these days that coming to church is a matter of getting in touch with ourselves or picking up a few tips to make our lives happier and more successful. God gets in the way. The cross is still a stumbling block. We would rather be consumers than disciples.

But Robert Wenz is not content to issue simplistic assertions about the current state of worship in our evangelical churches. Statistics, illustrations from contemporary life (including substantial support from secular periodicals, which often seem to have a strong grasp of the shift in evangelical worship), and nuanced interpretations of the data make this more than a polemic. Too often, our discussions of worship focus on practical matters: debates over styles, demographics, and methodologies. We need to correct the fundamental orientation, the author insists, with a rethinking of our entire theology of worship. That means a return to Scripture—not just as a source for illustrations in worship or support for the otherwise market-driven services, but as the formal principle from which we draw everything essential to our theory and practice.

Also of great significance is the balance this book offers between criticism and a constructive grid for a profoundly scriptural orientation, with the gospel and Christ at the center of every aspect of worship. We are such a pragmatic society that to even speak of a theology of worship sounds like an academic distraction from the truly important *practical* matters of immediate ministry needs. But, as the author makes abundantly clear, if there is no room for questions about God and his place in it all, why even advance to practical questions? What is worship, after all, without God?

Even evangelism and outreach take on the goal not of merely making converts, nor even disciples, but *worshipers*— those who will worship God in spirit and in truth. Being saved by grace alone liberates us from our deepest doubts, fears, and anxieties and makes us a congregation of grateful worshipers who, in turn, are changed in that very activity of worship. Instead of coming to church to be entertained, the believer is called to settle for nothing less than transformation; and this comes not through our own independent spir-

itual odyssey, but in our corporate relationship to and worship of the living Christ.

Going beyond truisms, Dr. Wenz provides us with a
provocative challenge that has the potential to transform the
ministry of churches across the country. When people start
getting bored with "relevance," the arguments in this book
will shout, "I told you so!" We can only hope that enough
people will read it before then.

Michael Horton

# PREFACE TO THE SECOND PRINTING

The evangelical subculture – like the world – has changed much since I first asked "Is there room for God in our worship?" The backdrop at that time was the church growth movement birthed in Southern California and flourishing in well-watered places like Willow Creek. At issue was the question of grace: Is God's amazing, transforming grace the theological foundation and spiritual inspiration for our worship or have we dumbed down or distorted the gospel for the sake of marketing?

Those questions are still valid even as some of the megachurches today are now being led by the sons of their founders. The stakes and pressures to fill huge arena-like churches have not abated, only increased.

But new pressures to compromise the gospel of grace alone through faith alone in Christ alone come from post-modernism and segments of the emergent church movement that at times seem to have capitulated to postmodernism. This movement may be lauded for some of its challenges to the church of modernity or for resurrecting ancient expressions of worship long overlooked by the church but, but if the Bible proponents are reading has been totally deconstructed by post-modernism and propositional truth has been invalidated, then what God are we worshipping?

So, while *Room for God?* addresses the issues of the church growth era that are still swirling, it also anticipates some of the questions the church must confront in a post-modern age, even as it has throughout history. You can read more at on my website ( www.totalworship.org ).

Dr. Bob Wenz

# INTRODUCTION

## Do You Know His Name?

We spend our entire lives acting out
our concept of God.
—Jack Taylor

On a recent trip to Mongolia, tourists—missionaries in disguise—encountered a curious mountain guide: "Do you know God? What is his Name?"[1] In what many Americans think of as the most remote place on earth, people wanted to know the name of God.

The history of missions is a history of encounters with tribes and people groups around the world that have an innate awareness of and interest in the true God and a desire to know his name. Any Christian who has been enriched by Don Richardson's fine work, *Eternity in Their Hearts*, knows that the evidence for such a universal awareness of a god is demonstrated around the world.

Although most anthropology textbooks acknowledge religion as universal,[2] we Christians understand the questions are critical because we believe that the question of which god we worship is of eternal, not just societal, significance. Moreover, as Christians we understand that the universal propensity to worship is part of how God created us: "He has also set eternity in the hearts of men" (Eccles. 3:11).

If worship of a god is a universal phenomenon, then two questions confront each of us:

> Do I worship the right God?
> Do I worship the right God the right way?

Millions of Americans make claims to pollsters about religious faith and practice, but we must question how such a society can also be in moral decline. If 95 percent of Americans say they believe in God, we must ask, "Which god?" If only about half of those people regularly express that faith in God, we must wonder if they are worshiping in the right way (or in any way!). We must agree, at least in part, with Martin Marty, who says that "our biggest problem is not secular humanism, but interest in religion that doesn't turn into commitment in everyday life."[3]

Many Americans live out a form of practical atheism. We are double-minded.

Evangelicals, a group variously numbered from forty to eighty million in the United States, are not immune to this double-mindedness; we just manifest different symptoms. We have not abandoned the Christian faith while we go on professing faith in God. Instead, we have embraced a mutant, human-centered Christianity while we go on professing faith in God. We seem as unaware of our double-mindedness as anyone else.

We must return to those same two questions: Are we worshiping the right God? Are we worshiping the right God in the right way? Before we answer too quickly, we need to take a careful look at our evangelical faith today.

PART **1**

# THE TRAP
# OF HUMAN-CENTERED
# CHRISTIANITY

# WORSHIP IN THE CHURCH GROWTH ERA

For the sort of people who like this
sort of thing, this is the sort of thing that
sort of people will like.
—Abraham Lincoln

## Asking the Right Questions

The *People's Almanac* a few years ago argued that the world's strangest religion was the cargo cult found on several islands in the southwest Pacific. During World War II the islanders discovered crates of cargo, floating debris from ships sunk in naval combat, washed up on their shore. The islanders marveled at this provision from an unknown source and concluded that the cargo came from a deity across the waters. They learned that military units received cargo, and that this was (seemingly mysteriously) connected with radio towers. Though they had no long-range radios, they erected simulated radio towers in hopes that the cargo god would be gracious and keep sending cargo. The islanders were not concerned with the theology of the matter—whether this was the true God and whether they were worshiping him in the right way. They were not interested in asking the right

19

questions about God. They cared only for what the cargo god could provide them via the currents of the Pacific Ocean.

If the islanders were not interested in theological questions, we certainly should be. The exclusive nature of the Christian faith we profess presses us to ask not just the two basic questions, but some related questions as well:

Is it possible to worship the true God?
Who is the god that we worship and call God?
Why do we worship God and not the gods?
Do we worship this right God in the right way?

These questions, valid in any era, are crucial today in light of the trends rippling through the evangelical subculture—trends put into motion by the church growth movement, now twenty years old.[1] The trend of applying certain principles, especially marketing principles, to the church has brought a fresh understanding and impetus to the church's task and tools of evangelism. The church growth movement has served a valid and worthwhile service by helping many churches to refocus on the task of outreach.

I have become increasingly concerned, however, with a number of the manifestations of what John MacArthur calls the "pragmatic approach" to church growth—"seeker" and "seeker-sensitive services" or "user-friendly churches."[2] I can easily agree with much of what MacArthur has written about the error of pragmatism—that it is prone to value methodologies above biblical truth.

However, I will also argue that Paul instructed the church in the basics of seeker-sensitive worship. After all, Paul was being sensitive to the unbeliever by seeking to be all things to all people to win them to Christ. What balanced Paul's pragmatism was his commitment to please God rather than people (2 Cor. 5:9) and his renunciation of "secret and shameful ways" that are deceptive and "distort the word of God" (2 Cor. 4:2).

The trend toward consumer orientation in evangelicalism is advanced by the ubiquitous conferences and seminars that teach churches how to attract worshipers, especially baby boomers. To become a megachurch (or at least a successful church) in today's marketplace, we are told, a church must become consumer-oriented; must offer modern facilities, ample parking, maximum program options, low-commitment demands, excellent child care; must meet needs; and must carefully avoid religious jargon.

But some churches have gone beyond being sensitive to unbelievers to accommodating them at the cost of violating biblical truth. Even where pragmatism has not been openly embraced, it has created a dangerous undercurrent that threatens the church. We must strive to put the church growth movement into perspective by looking at several of the dangers inherent in an indiscriminate adherance to church growth thinking.

## The Dangers of the Church Growth Movement

### Asking the Wrong Questions

The greatest dangers of the market-driven, consumer-oriented, or seeker-sensitive ministries come from the wrong questions inherent in bringing a marketing approach to the church. It seems some churches have bypassed the basic questions about God and adopted a new set of foundational questions by which they define their ministries. These questions are the ones made famous by the door-to-door surveys conducted by some churches.[3] They are also base-level questions, but the line of enquiry is different and dangerous:

What do you want in a church?
What kind of church might you be willing to attend?
What kinds of things in the church keep you away?

These questions, revolving around the "you" who are surveyed, reveal a drift toward a human-centered Christianity.

To my knowledge no church marketing leader has yet asked, "What kind of God do you want?" or "What kind of God would you be willing to worship?" Yet, in some cases (see chap. 4), providing the kind of God the customer prefers may be camouflaged by a thin veneer of spirituality. Moreover, asking the wrong questions shifts the focus to "felt needs" rather than to people's real needs. Perhaps these leaders assume felt needs and real needs are the same.

It may be valuable for a church to study the demographics of its community and even to know that unchurched people are concerned about well-kept facilities, adequate parking, good child care, and remaining anonymous in the church. We must remove the human stumbling blocks that keep the unchurched away. We must not try to remove the spiritual stumbling blocks that are inherent in a gospel that confronts sinful humanity with its real need. Striving to create a church that people want may produce a church that is not at all what God wants.

### The Market-Driven Church

Although the church growth movement has helped many churches think creatively and sharpen their emphasis on outreach, there exists the serious danger of the church becoming market driven. We must exercise creativity and wisdom in our outreach ministry, but we also must guard against allowing marketing to dominate our thinking. The church growth movement will have done a great disservice to the church if the result is to rewrite our doctrine. One-third of our finest evangelical college students, surveyed at the most recent Urbana Conference, do not believe that God will send anyone to hell. Where did they learn that? In their market-driven evangelical churches. On the advice of church marketing experts, many churches have jettisoned the biblical teaching about hell. Obviously, as some reason, teaching the doctrine of eternal punishment will stunt or impair church growth.

## The Success Syndrome

Paradoxically, one of the greatest dangers of the market-driven church may be that it is often successful. The success orientation of our culture has seeped into the church, bringing with it the dangerous assumption that success equates with truth. If numeric growth, buildings, television ratings, and millions of dollars raised are all criteria for success, then we have adopted our yardsticks from our culture and not from God's Word. One of the pioneers of marketing the church, Robert Schuller, responded to my questions about a theological statement that he made on his "Hour of Power" broadcast by saying that his "new theology" is proven correct by the success of his ministry.[4] Yet such reasoning is clearly false. To equate success with truth is analogous to saying that because a fast-food chain is successful, its food is nutritious. Marketing the church is subject to the same dangerous pitfall. The market-driven church may succeed at giving people what they want, but may depend too heavily on carnal values or spiritually ignorant people to prescribe for the church its ministry and perhaps it message.

The rise of some highly visible market-driven churches puts enormous pressure on other churches to be successful—that is, to become megachurches. All pastors want their churches to grow, but this "success syndrome" has caused many churches to evaluate pastors in terms of numerical growth of the church rather than the biblical call to faithfulness. In this environment many effective and faithful men and women of God are found wanting. We can attribute the high attrition and turnover rates in the ministry to the success syndrome. When pastors cannot duplicate the success of their colleagues, they are replaced as fast as are the managers of last-place teams in the major leagues. One observer, Ronald Weinelt of the Association for Battered Clergy, has said, "'A lot of us pastors are making ourselves sick and crazy trying to figure out how to score with yuppie boomers. . . .' Many pastors function around some addictive patterns: 'workaholism, perfectionism, control, success-orientation, domination by statistics, or a need to be caretakers, people-pleasers, fixers, and rescuers.' . . . 'That's a real crazy maker.' . . . Pastors are also frustrated by parishioners' decreasing commitment, but increasing expectation of church leaders."[5]

### Evangelical Consumerism

In a highly competitive religious marketplace geared to addressing the felt needs of the public, it should surprise no one if church growth principles have had a great impact on those already in the church, an impact perhaps greater on Christians than on non-Christians. A marketing approach applied to a narcissistic age has transformed countless evangelicals into church consumers. It has even made some into church connoisseurs.

The story of Saddleback Valley Community Church, an outstanding and solidly evangelical church in Southern California, illustrates this concern. The church was planted in the early 1980s and its marketing strategy was geared to reaching "Saddleback Sam," the demographically defined, quintessential, unchurched baby boomer in the Saddleback Valley. During the first few years of effective outreach ministry, 75 to 80 percent of the church's growth came from the conversion of formerly unchurched Saddleback Sams. The church did an excellent job of targeting and reaching many unchurched people who have come to Christ! The church and Rick Warren, the senior pastor, have maintained a strong biblical orientation and orthodoxy.

However, as the church has grown it has been "discovered" by a host of baby-boomer evangelical consumers who see this as a "better church." The latest data suggest that only about a fourth of the church's growth comes from unchurched people. The rest of the growth comes from people in search of a church that caters to their needs more effectively, a pattern common among evangelical baby boomers.[6] Marketing approaches, when they are applied to the "me first" generation, appear to have ensnared many evangelicals into becoming church consumers.

One manifestation of evangelical consumerism is growing and certainly unhealthy. In large metropolitan areas where there are high-profile megachurches, consumerism has spawned commuterism. Perhaps the best way to describe commuterism is with a fictional composite example.

Tom and Sue live in Hometown, suburb of a major American city. They commute some distance to work, so they think little of commuting thirty miles on Sunday to First Evangelical Megachurch of Churchville. They think it is the best church in the area. The pastor is well known and the church offers many special ministries. However, because they don't live in Churchville, Tom and Sue cannot be involved at FEM-COC other than on Sunday morning and for occasional special events. They cannot participate in a small group, even if they had a free night. In fact, Tom and Sue don't really like the community of Churchville. They are not sure they would want to be in a small group with Churchville people. Consequently, they don't share in a vision for ministry or for reaching the people of Churchville. If we pressed Tom and Sue, they might admit that the only thing they actually know about Churchville is how to get to the campus of FEMCOC and where the good restaurants are in the neighborhood of the church. But because they leave Hometown in order to worship in Churchville, they cannot have much of a vested interest or involvement in ministry to Hometown. I know dozens of Toms and Sues—commuter Christians who exhibit one form of consumerism.

Yet another expression of consumerism is the multiple-church single. Single people make up nearly 40 percent of the church, and many of them have become multiple-church consumers: that is, they consider themselves members of several churches at the same time. They rotate their attendance from church to church according to what activities are being held, who they are dating, and who is preaching. They have groups of friends or acquaintances in each church and this gives them a sense of belonging, but they are unlikely to actually join one church. (This behavior pattern may change when people marry and have children; children need a stable church environment, as their parents learn.)

## The Baby-Boomer Craze

The marketplace is bursting with and seemingly obsessed with baby boomers. Baby boomers are such a significant group numerically that we cannot ignore them, and it is natural to want to market the church to them. But, as a group, they demand excellence, multiple options, and that they be catered to in exchange for their religious patronage. We must contend with the reality that boomers have reduced attention spans, lack loyalty, and are reluctant to make commitments.[7]

Baby boomers present a threefold concern. First, there is the practical danger of creating a church that seemingly ignores everyone not born between 1945 and 1968. Second, reaching unchurched baby boomers by meeting their felt needs may prove to be less difficult than trying to keep them in the church, for keeping them requires perpetually catering to their felt needs and their growing expectations. Third, when we successfully reach baby boomers with a solid church marketing program, we still must determine how to safeguard the church from the me-generation values they carry with them.

*Containment!*

The most subtle danger of the market-driven church is that a consumer orientation can then move through the church like a computer virus infecting program after program. Over time, preaching may focus almost entirely on our human needs and the problems we face (e.g., time management, self-esteem, anxiety, compulsive behavior, successful marriage and parenting). Our doctrine may focus on ourselves and our felt needs rather than on God. Sin, for example, becomes "not thinking we are worthy of God's love," and grace becomes a general principle of God's love. The result is that many evangelicals no longer believe and proclaim a God who could ever really send someone to hell. (And even if he were going to send some monstrously evil people to hell, it is best not mention something as confrontational as the judgment of God in polite society.) Finally, we evolve into people who worship God not for who he is but for how abundantly he has blessed us—especially with health and wealth. We have arrived at the front steps of the "Church of What Have You Done for Me Lately?"

When everything in the church is geared to humanity and perceived human needs, this attitude will invade our sanctuaries and our worship. Using practical creative approaches to reach the unchurched is not wrong, but a pragmatic, market-driven church will ultimately have market-driven and human-centered worship.

## Go and Make Disciples

If marketing the church has replaced making disciples as the primary strategy for fulfilling the Great Commission, then we have abandoned the truth of God's Word and are doomed to fail. Discipleship is always a costly process. It is a call to the cross, where we must give up our agenda and embrace the agenda of our Savior. It is the failure of the church to make disciples that underlies the need for church growth strategies. It is much easier to run programs than to make disciples.

Jesus was never willing to compromise the call to life-changing discipleship in favor of a larger market share and the appearance of successful ministry. We are reminded of John 6:

> Jesus said to them, "I tell you the truth, unless you eat the flesh of the Son of Man and drink his blood, you have no life in you."
>
> On hearing it, many of his disciples said, "This is a hard teaching. Who can accept it?"
> Aware that his disciples were grumbling about this, Jesus said to them, "Does this offend you?"
>
> From this time many of his disciples turned back and no longer followed him.
> "You do not want to leave too, do you?" Jesus asked the Twelve.
> Simon Peter answered him, "Lord, to whom shall we go? You have the words of eternal life. We believe and know that you are the Holy One of God." [vv. 53, 60–61, 66–68]

Making disciples differs from successfully marketing the church. Jesus never retreated from confronting his listeners with the truth for fear that some might leave and go elsewhere. He never attempted to bait his followers with a message geared to their needs, only to switch his message as he led his followers along an escalating path of actual costs.

Marketing may succeed in bringing unchurched people into the church, but if there is ultimately no difference in their lives—and studies show that the average churched persons in the United States differ little from their unchurched counterparts in conduct, divorce rate, ethics, or understanding of God—then all we have done can hardly be called success. We have not converted people. We have not made disciples. We have merely turned unchurched people into churched people—people who attend our meetings and inflate our statistics and perhaps our egos. In chapter 7 we will consider more fully the relationship between worship and making disciples. It will suffice here to note that becoming a true worshiper of the true God is to become a disciple, one who lays down his or her own baggage and by faith takes up the cross of the Lord Jesus.

## The Current Evangelical Environment

In the 1990s, a decade that emphasizes marketing the church to baby boomers, countless churches in the United States are arguing the merits of traditional and contemporary worship or debating the place of seeker or seeker-sensitive ministries in their churches. Perhaps these debates are too frequently divisive and destructive because we have not clearly addressed the underlying issue of what it means to worship God. It is important to help the contemporary church recognize that the real issues involved go well beyond the style or volume or instrumentation of church music. Although there are many excellent books about worship in the marketplace, they are often "how-to" books or "how-we" books that tend to focus on how others have developed successful worship ministries. Because success is usually defined in terms of the numbers (or increased numbers) of worshipers who consume the services, we are confronted by the troubling realization that many evangelicals see worship (and not just evangelism) as market-driven or consumer-oriented. What often seems to be lacking is a counterbalancing focus on the God-centeredness of worship.

If worship is a central "product" of the church, we must come to grips with the truth that God himself and not the worshiper is the real consumer of our worship. Can church worship services and ministries forged on the anvil of consumer surveys and marketing principles lead us to truly worship God?

## Developing a Proper Perspective on Worship

There are, of course, two distinctly different ways of looking at worship—God's perspective and our own human perspective. Developing an understanding of these distinct perspectives is foundational to gaining a strategic grasp of the church's ministry of worship.

Perhaps this can be illustrated on a different level. My wife and I have a daughter and a son, Lauren and Andrew, whom we adopted as infants in 1985 and 1990. In each case, the adoption process was agonizingly slow, time consuming, and quite costly, but wonderfully rewarding! Consequently, adoption has taken on a special meaning that we cannot help but savor when we encounter any mention of adoption in the Bible.

Our appreciation for the adoption process began to grow from the moment we initiated the process. "Our agency is not in the business of providing children for couples who desire them. The agency is here to provide homes and families for children who need them," said our case worker when we commenced the first adoption in 1980. It was not what I was expecting to hear. I had always assumed only the perspective of the parents. I had not realized that adoptive parents and adopted children will forever see the process of adoption from two different perspectives.

For parents, adoptions happen because couples (and some single people) desire to have children and initiate the process. We parents see the long process through, pay the price, and bear the burden of nurture. We are also the ones who exulted in the day each child arrived and who hosted the celebrations. We sent adoption announcements to our friends and family and anyone else we could think of who might possibly be interested. We took the pictures and celebrated when each adoption was finalized in court.

For children, the adoptive process begins with a need for loving parents and a good home. Neither of my children initiated the process of adoption and neither has truly begun to comprehend it. No infant selects his or her adoptive family. The infants' contribution to the process was their need!

Granted, many couples have adopted children out of a loving response to the need of specific orphaned or abandoned children—even severely disabled children. Responses to a news report about a newborn abandoned in a dumpster attest to the number of people wanting to adopt needy little ones. But in the United States, where one infant is placed for every forty couples who have expressed a desire to adopt, there seems to be a lot more pent-up desire than needy children. So while there may be exceptions, the adoptive process generally begins with that parental desire God seems to have given to many.

In the parallel process of spiritual adoption, God initiated the process, waited patiently, paid all of the costs, and will ultimately finalize the adoption with a great celebration at the end of the age.

We, his adopted children, contributed to the process only our need. (Someone has rightly said that the only thing I contributed to my salvation was the sin that made it necessary.) In our spiritual adoption, God seeks and gains the worshipers he desires, and we gain the salvation we desperately need. Both the parent (the Father) and the adopted children share in and relish the beauty of the relationship; but from first to last, our adoption is a work of God's grace for his glory.

Similarly, Paul reminds us that "we are God's workmanship, created in Christ Jesus unto good works." Because God has adopted us into his family of worshipers, we cannot fully comprehend the cost—the cost of his only Son—or the patience of God in the process of adoption. It is a wonderful process that means God "has rescued us from the dominion of darkness and brought us into the kingdom of the Son he loves."

Although he responded to our great need, God ultimately adopted us out of his desire to receive worship. We come to understand that it is altogether fitting and proper for him to so desire to be worshiped as we grow in our understanding of his character and the nature of his deity. Jesus in the garden prayed, "And now, Father, glorify me in your presence with the glory I had with you before the world began" (John 17:5). The Son of God desired earnestly to return to his proper station in heaven so that he again might receive the worship that is rightfully his.

God has no need of worship or of the adopted children who might worship him. He is complete without us or our worship. His desire for worship is no indictment against his perfection—the triune God exists in the perfect eternal fellowship of Father, Son, and Holy Spirit. Yet, acting on his desire, God created all things for his pleasure and for the purpose of glorifying him. We are part of that creation for his pleasure and his glory.

So, while we have a need—a need for him and a need to worship him—our adoption into God's family of worshipers does not begin with our need but with God's desire to be worshiped. Certainly God's program for our adoption is an expression of infinite love and grace to our desperate need. We were still his spiritual enemies when he gave his son to die for us that we might also become sons and daughters.

As wonderful as it may be for us to be adopted into God's eternal family of worshipers, worship is and must be God-centered because it begins with God's proper desire to be glorified, not with our need.

## God-Centered versus Human-Centered Worship

Worship should never be human-centered and must always be God-centered. True worshipers understand this and view worship from this perspective. They approach God because God is worthy of worship, even if he had not redeemed or adopted us. At the end of the age, even those who have scorned him will acknowledge his lordship, not because they have received the blessing of adoption (they have not) but because he is Lord!

In the process of adopting us as worshipers and children, God has so poured out his blessings on us that needy and naturally self-centered children may get caught up in the blessings of God rather than in the God who blesses. Worship risks becoming human-centered when the focus of our relationship with God fails to rise above our needs, our feelings, or the blessing we receive when we worship the One who blesses. This danger is revealed by the questions we often ask about how "we enjoyed the worship service," what "we got out of a sermon," and whether or not "we were fed."

The nature of this potential can be seen in the Psalms:

> Bless the LORD, O my soul!
> And all that is within me, bless his holy name.
> Bless the LORD, O my soul,
> and forget not all his benefits. [Ps. 103:1–2 KJV]

Because God has blessed us so richly, it is easy to become fixated on those blessings. Let us recall that in the Bible the word *blessing,* when used of God, always refers to something tangible (though not always material) that God does or has done for us. When the Bible speaks of man blessing God, it almost always refers to something verbal. It is a remarkable trade—God receives our words of blessing, we receive the tangible fruit called blessing.

True worship, however, is not related to our subjective response to worship. Stephen Charnock cuts to the core of the issue: "When we believe that we should be satisfied rather than God glorified in our worship then we put God below ourselves as though He had been made for us rather than that we had been made for Him." Charnock's choice of the word *satisfied* is important. Many people in our evangelical churches seem more concerned with their satisfaction in worship than with God's glorification. The popularity of some churches or ministries seems to derive from their emphasis on making worship rewarding or satisfying. It even seems that we have passively trained people (by repeated reinforcement) that worship is principally a process or an exercise whose purpose is to secure the rewards God offers to those who seek him.

It is a subtle trap: whenever we insist or require that worship be _____ [fill in your own adjective], we are drawn into human-centered worship. It doesn't matter which adjective we choose, the mere process of evaluating worship on our terms makes it human-centered.

Worship should be exciting, edifying, and even satisfying. Proper worship always will be. If it is not, then either we have not worshiped the right God or we have not worshiped in the right way. If we come to worship looking to be _____ [the adjective you chose], then our worship is destined, even doomed, to be human-centered, not God-centered. The result will be that our worship experience will disappoint us because it will not have been what we thought it should have been.

However, when we worship God with no agenda except to glorify him (his agenda for our worship), then we will enter into a fellowship with God that fills us far more than our agenda could have prescribed. Without question, his invitation for us to seek him by faith is accompanied by the announcement of reward: "He rewards those who earnestly seek him" (Heb. 11:6). Here is a divine paradox along the order of what Jesus said—"He who loses his life for my sake will find it"—because anyone who comes to God with no agenda except to glorify God will receive "from the fullness of his grace . . . one blessing after another" (John 1:16). So it is not a surprise that the psalmist could write in the same song, "Bless the LORD, O my soul" and "forget not all his benefits."

## The Human-Centered Gospel

There is another paradox. Proper worship must be God-centered, yet the gospel of Jesus Christ itself centers on the sinful race of Adam. God manifested his love for us and his desire for us by initiating a dramatic program to adopt us as his children and to enlist us as his worshipers. The gospel is about what God has done for us. The gospel is about who we can be in Christ—the children of God.

But the goal of God's program to adopt us as his children is nothing less than to transform a sinful race of Satan's children into the likeness of Jesus Christ (Rom. 8:29). The change is drastic! God wants to change us from selfish people into people who "no longer live for themselves but for him who died for them" (2 Cor. 5:15). The goal of the church is to radically change contemporary men and women.

The task of attracting and enlisting unchurched people (formerly called "unsaved") to become worshipers of the true God is the vital process of conversion: they "turned to God from idols to serve the living and true God" (1 Thess. 1:9). Conversion is the product of a human-centered gospel preached to change us into God-centered worshipers.

As we proclaim enthusiastically a human-centered gospel, we must make sure we proclaim the whole gospel:

God loves us!
*But we are the sinful children of Satan.*

God loves us!
*But we must change!*
God wants to adopt us into his family as his children!
*But it means we must die to our natural family and lifestyle.*
God has given us a means of salvation!
*And what we're saved from is nothing less than hell.*

There is a temptation to employ a form of the bait-and-switch tactic in the church. The temptation is to switch the gospel, either because we feel some ambiguity in proclaiming a genuinely paradoxical message or because we are afraid that part of the gospel is too confrontational. It is easier to preach just one half: God loves you. The challenge of maintaining a balance is a great one. Our failure to maintain a balanced presentation of the gospel that confronts our real needs, not just our felt needs, as well as God's gracious remedy, has resulted in a human-centered gospel that has led to human-centered Christianity.

## Human-Centered Christianity

The danger of any shift of focus away from a God-centered faith—done under the banner of proclaiming the gospel—is that we end up not only with a human-centered gospel but also with market-driven ministries, consumer-oriented churches, and, ultimately, human-centered Christianity.

It is little wonder that Francis Schaeffer feared that evangelicalism was being reduced to only two central values, personal peace and affluence. Evangelicals, he said, aspire only for their own personal world to be stable and at peace and to have enough money to enjoy that peaceful personal world. Kenneth S. Kantzer, a senior editor of *Christianity Today*, recently reiterated that evangelicals have forgotten the privilege of "sharing in [Jesus'] sufferings" and are preoccupied with wealth and health.[8] Human-centered Christianity focuses on the blessing of God.

In our emphasis on the blessings of the Christian life, we have lost sight of the primary reason we worship the God of the Bible. We worship him because he is the true God. We worship him because he is holy. We worship him because he is the sovereign God who will cause every knee to bow and every tongue to acknowledge that he is Lord. We worship him because he will judge the nations and send the ungodly to hell.

God's blessings stimulate our praise and worship, but his blessings are not the reason he is to be worshiped. Our current focus appears to be shifting away from worship based upon the character of God revealed propositionally in the Bible to worship based upon our experience. It appears that the consumer-oriented church is only a predictable consequence of a community of faith that has embraced with head and heart the existentialism of the culture.

Connie Chung of NBC News interviewed Billy Graham for the "Today" show on his sixty-fifth birthday. She commended him for being the "most successful evangelist" in history. Graham quickly reminded her that God does not call us to be successful, only faithful. With that exhortation in mind, I hope in the following chapters to summon the evangelical church to faithfulness to our calling as worshipers—God-centered worshipers in an age given to religious hedonism.

# WORSHIPING THE RIGHT GOD

Lord, to whom shall we go?
You have the words of eternal life. We
believe and know that you are the Holy
One of God.
—Simon Peter
(John 6:68–69)

## Alien Beauty

In Lechuguilla Cave near Carlsbad, New Mexico, geologists and spelunkers have discovered a beauty beyond comprehension. One geologist, quoted in the Detroit *Free Press,* described it this way: "Everything is alien . . . so beautiful that you just have to leave. You just can't take it."[1] Words cannot adequately describe what these geologists saw. Pictures are better, but pictures are two-dimensional and also inadequate.

The geologists unknowingly provide us an insight into the basic issue of why we worship God. Those who experienced the overwhelming beauty of the cave remind us that we worship a God of alien beauty. *Holiness* is a word found in the Bible to describe this quality of God, a beauty that both attracts and repels. It is a beauty that is beyond human adjec-

tives and superlatives. It is also a beauty so foreign to us that
we too must "leave" because we "just can't take it."

We encounter the alien beauty of God in the dramatic
account in which John seeks to describe what he sees in
heaven:

> At once I was in the Spirit, and there before me was a throne
> in heaven with someone sitting on it. And the one who sat
> there had the appearance of jasper and carnelian. A rainbow,
> resembling an emerald, encircled the throne. Surrounding
> the throne were twenty-four other thrones, and seated on
> them were twenty-four elders. They were dressed in white
> and had crowns of gold on their heads. From the throne came
> flashes of lightning, rumblings and peals of thunder. Before
> the throne, seven lamps were blazing. These are the seven
> spirits of God. Also before the throne there was what looked
> like a sea of glass, clear as crystal. [Rev. 4:2–6]

John tries to describe God but falls short. Words cannot capture
the vision. An alien beauty draws us toward God, but an
awesome presence overwhelms our senses and gives us pause
as we see a glimpse of "the splendor of holiness" (Ps. 29:2).

God's holiness is a compelling beauty; but it is also a
repelling beauty. Isaiah cried, "Woe to me!" because he had
seen the Lord. Moses longed to see the glory of God, yet
turned his head as God passed by. We worship God because
he is holy. We flee from God because he is holy.

### Why We Worship God

With Revelation 4 as background, we can try to answer
the question of why we worship God. If we are to have a
right understanding of the worship of God, we must carry
the discussion back to this most basic issue. If there is a god,
then he must have certain distinguishing qualities. We worship the God of the Bible because we have determined that

he is the true God, the God who is worthy of our worship based upon his qualifications for deity.

This chapter is not an exhaustive treatment of the existence and attributes of God. None of the fine systematic theologies, nor Stephen Charnock's two definitive volumes on the attributes of God, are in danger of being rivaled here.[2] We need, however, to reaffirm our understanding of God because that understanding serves as a reference point to measure any drift from the biblical call to worship the true God in the right way.

## God Is the Holy One

God is holy!

That God is holy is the sufficient reason given by the Bible for worshiping God. In saying that God is holy, we envelop all the essential attributes of God that make him worthy of worship and praise and honor and glory! We often think of holiness as moral perfection, but God's holiness encompasses far more than his moral perfection. He is morally perfect, to be sure. But the holiness of God can perhaps best be defined as his *otherness*. He is alien to us because his essence or being—what makes him God—differs from ours. His essence is alien, yet beautiful.

Our finite minds cannot comprehend him. We do not even possess the mental categories or words to accurately or adequately describe him. We worship him simply because he is what he is. We should not, therefore, find it surprising that he uses the name "I AM WHO I AM" (Hebrew: YHWH or Yahweh; see Exod 3:14). John the apostle is so overtaken by a revelation of God's holiness, glory, and majesty that John's words fall short of giving an adequate description, even under the inspiration of the Holy Spirit. In 2 Corinthians 12:4, Paul reminds us that on the writers of Scripture are restricted concerning what they are permitted to reveal about heaven! And, of course, there is a limit to what we can comprehend with

our finite minds. Revelation takes us only so far and leaves us
at times with more questions than answers. Nonetheless, Revelation 4:6–8 makes clear the first reason why we worship:

> In the center, around the throne, were four living creatures,
> and they were covered with eyes, in front and in back. The
> first living creature was like a lion, the second was like an
> ox, the third had a face like a man, the fourth was like a fly-
> ing eagle. Each of the four living creatures had six wings and
> was covered with eyes all around, even under his wings. Day
> and night they never stop saying:
>
> > "Holy, holy, holy
> > is the Lord God Almighty,
> > who was, and is, and is to come."

The holiness of God encompasses a constellation of qualities
that distinguish him from all of his creation and make him
worthy of our worship.

### God Has Unique Attributes

John confirms in Revelation 4:9–11 that we are worshiping the right God when we worship the God of the Bible and
that he alone is worthy of worship because he alone has the
qualifications:

> Whenever the living creatures give glory, honor and thanks
> to him who sits on the throne and who lives for ever and ever,
> the twenty-four elders fall down before him who sits on the
> throne, and worship him who lives for ever and ever. They
> lay their crowns before the throne and say:
>
> > "You are worthy, our Lord and God,
> >     to receive glory and honor and power,
> > for you created all things,
> >     and by your will they were created
> >     and have their being."

In addition to the otherness of God, there are four distinct qualities that, for lack of a better phrase, "make God God." Theologians have traditionally classified the attributes of God into two categories. *Communicable* attributes are those attributes God shares to some degree with his creation: love, truthfulness, goodness, righteousness, justice, to list a few. God's *noncommunicable* attributes include his omniscience, omnipotence, omnipresence, and changelessness, attributes God does not share with his creation.

We can think of God's attributes in three categories: the essential attributes that make the God of the Bible the true God, the attributes that he alone possesses (incommunicable), and the attributes that he shares with his creation (communicable), attributes that flow out of his essential divine qualities.

## Illustration 2.1
### *The Attributes of God*

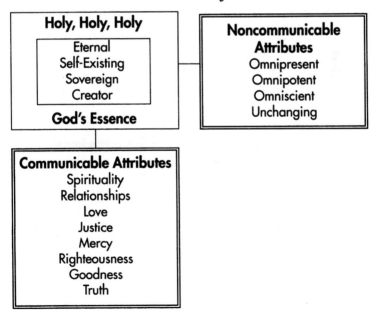

**Holy, Holy, Holy**

Eternal
Self-Existing
Sovereign
Creator

**God's Essence**

**Noncommunicable Attributes**
Omnipresent
Omnipotent
Omniscient
Unchanging

**Communicable Attributes**
Spirituality
Relationships
Love
Justice
Mercy
Righteousness
Goodness
Truth

Of the four qualities that define God's otherness, he is, first, eternal. The angels are quick to acknowledge his eternal nature: "Who was, and is, and is to come" (Rev. 4:8). His eternal nature is the logical key to the other essential divine attributes. An eternal Being must by logic and definition be before all other things and the source of all other things. The eternal God is outside the limits of time, which he also created.

If we see God's glorious holiness as the shell that envelops all his divine attributes, then his eternality is the nucleus from which the other divine attributes derive (see illustration 2.1).

Because God is eternal, he is by logical necessity self-existing. He was not created, he did not evolve, and he did not mutate from something into God. He has always been. He has always been God. Everything that exists must be either self-existing or contingent upon someone or something else—caused or uncaused. When we think in these categories we recognize that because God is eternal, he must be uncaused and must be the uncaused cause of everything else. Everything owes its existence to God: "by your will they . . . have their being" (Rev. 4:11).

This in turn establishes him as sovereign over everything. Sovereignty means that God can do anything he wills to do. Sovereignty also means that we can do only what God allows us to do. The same holds true for all of God's creation, even the fallen angels and their leader, Satan (see Job 1). We have "free will," but our free will is ultimately limited by God's sovereignty.

Because God is sovereign, by definition he possesses specific attributes. He has infinite power (omnipotence). Because he is sovereign, he can know whatever he wills to know, possessing knowledge (and the ability to know) beyond limit. This infinite knowledge allows God to know simultaneously the number of hairs on the head and the thoughts inside the head of every person. The Sovereign is also beyond spatial limitation on his being—he is infinite and present everywhere he chooses to be.

As the eternal sovereign God, he is the creator of all things: "for you created all things, and by your will they were created" (Rev. 4:11). God, the sovereign, eternal, self-existing One, willed everything else into being.

That God is the creator of all things is no abstract truth. If he is creator of all things, then he is my creator and I am accountable to my creator as his creation.

Remember, if there is a God, he must by definition be the eternal, uncaused cause of all things. If there is a God worthy of our worship, then he must be more than even the loftiest mental projections of man. He must be other than us and transcend our ability to comprehend him. If we understand his holiness as his essential quality that makes him other than us, we can understand why John's report of worship from heaven begins: "Holy, holy, holy is the Lord, God Almighty!"

The God of the Bible is the true God because he fits the definition of a God worthy of worship. He possesses all the defining qualities of God.

### Illustration 2.2
#### *The Divine Essence*

| | |
|---|---|
| **Holy** | "Holy, holy, holy!" |
| **Eternal** | "Who was and is and is to come" |
| **Self-Existing** | "[In you] all things have their being" |
| **Sovereign** | "Worthy to receive power" |
| | "By your will they were created" |
| **Creator** | "For you created all things" |

Because he possesses these qualities, we understand that God is other than us: he is holy. The God of the Bible is presented as the only worthy object of worship because he is other, very much other, than us (see illustration 2.3).

## Illustration 2.3
### *The Otherness of God*

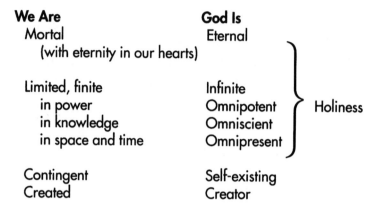

**We Are**
Mortal
  (with eternity in our hearts)

Limited, finite
  in power
  in knowledge
  in space and time

Contingent
Created

**God Is**
Eternal

Infinite
Omnipotent
Omniscient
Omnipresent

Self-existing
Creator

Holiness

In a single statement, the angels in heaven have affirmed that there is sufficient reason to worship this God of the Bible.

As Christians, we seek to worship the true God, the one deity who is qualified (worthy) to be worshiped. The deity we worship, the God revealed in the Bible, is worthy to be worshiped because that God possesses all the qualifications for deity that are articulated by the angels of heaven and demanded by reason.

### *God Is the Qualifier*

John's revelation suggests a third reason that God is worthy of our worship: God has qualified us to worship him through the cross of Christ.

You are worthy . . .
because you were slain,
  and with your blood you purchased men for God
  from every tribe and language and people and nation.

You have made them to be a kingdom and priests to serve
    our God
and they will reign on the earth. [Rev. 5:9–10]

I will amplify this reason for worshiping God later, but it
needs to be mentioned. We need to distinguish this reason
from the first two on one important point: although God is
worthy of worship, we are not worthy to be worshipers. It is,
therefore, all the more fitting for us to worship him because
he has made it possible through the person and work of his
Son. We worship him because he is the qualifier of human
worshipers.

## No Reason Not to Worship God

Because God has called us to worship him and in Christ
has qualified us to be his worshipers, we have no valid reason for not worshiping him:

For since the creation of the world God's invisible qualities—
his eternal power and divine nature [i.e., holiness]—have
been clearly seen, being understood from what has been
made, so that men are without excuse. [Rom. 1:20]

The true God, whose essential divine nature is encompassed
by his holiness, has given us sufficient reason and evidence
to worship him by revealing in his creation both his sovereign
power and his holy eternal divine nature (his otherness).
Paul affirms that we have been given sufficient reason to
worship the God of the Bible as the right God.

Paul also gives us valuable insight concerning why men
and women worship the wrong God. Imbedded in these few
verses from Romans 1 are three important principles regard-
ing worship of the true God:

. . . men who suppress the truth by their wickedness, since what may be known about God is plain to them, because God has made it plain to them. [vv. 18–19]

For although they knew God, they neither glorified him as God nor gave thanks to him, but their thinking became futile and their foolish hearts were darkened. [v. 21]

Although they claimed to be wise, they became fools and exchanged the glory of the immortal God for images made to look like mortal man and birds and animals and reptiles. [vv. 22–23]

First, God has provided us with sufficient evidence to seek the right god to worship from among all gods. The sufficient evidence is before us because God has made himself known to us in part. Theologians call this the general revelation of God. But while theologians agree that general revelation is not sufficient to bring a person to salvation, they seem to overlook—amidst the various arguments for the existence of God[3]—that general revelation gives us sufficient insight to reject all the wrong and inadequate gods. General revelation may not take us to God—special revelation does that—but it takes us away from all that is not God.

Paul underscored the evidence of the eternality of God, a reality beyond the experience (but not beyond the ability to reason and conceptualize) of finite humankind. If there is a god, such a god by definition would have to be eternal. If there is a god who is eternal and before all things, then this god must be the antecedent and the creator of all things. If a being is not eternal, then that being is categorically disqualified from being considered the true God.

Paul clearly stated that the true God can be identified by a process of elimination: The right god to worship is the one who existed before all things and created all things. Therefore, any god that was created by man is clearly disqualified from consideration as deity.

Second, Paul implies that gratitude and ingratitude represent an important fork in the road to knowing God. Ingratitude (Rom. 1:21) is the point at which many turn away from the path that leads to the true God. Ingratitude leads people away from God, but it is just the first step away from God. It leads to the denial that we are created; then to the denial that God is Creator; and then to the denial that we are dependent upon him as Creator for everything. This path leads ultimately to the denial that we are accountable to God for how we live the lives he created for us and use the things he created and gave us. Alternatively, the first step a person makes toward God in worship is to thank him as the creator for all that he created (or at least for all that God created that gives benefit or pleasure to that individual). Yet, thankfulness expresses more than an appreciation for things created. It also expresses an awareness and appreciation of the inherent stratified relationship of dependence of a created being to his or her Creator.

Third, Paul implies that people also turn away from their search for the true God because of the issue of holiness: God is holy and we are not (Rom. 1:18). We began this chapter by focusing on the alien beauty of God—beauty so splendid that we are both repelled by it and attracted to it. Because our thinking is distorted by the fall, we seem to be more repelled by God's alien beauty than attracted to it.

This misdirected search for the true God leads people to embrace false gods, gods that by definition are not God because they are part of the creation, even as we are. "They exchanged the truth of God for a lie, and worshiped and served created things rather than the Creator—who is forever praised. Amen" (Rom. 1:25). Gods manufactured out of the human imagination—the god of Mormonism, the god of Jehovah's Witnesses, Baal, Shiva—are false gods.

## Illustration 2.4
### *The Transcendent God*

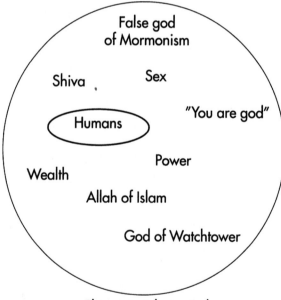

**Holy
Eternal
Sovereign
Self-Existing
Creator**

The God who exists
outside space and time

False god
of Mormonism

Shiva          Sex

"You are god"

Humans

Wealth          Power

Allah of Islam

God of Watchtower

The material, created
world of space and time

We worship the God of the Bible because he is the God who transcends our sphere of creation, whose essence is other than ours, who is holy. We worship God because he alone transcends the created universe. We worship God because he is eternal and transcends the created, time-bound world. Nothing that is part of the creation is worthy of our worship. By definition, then, we can identify God as that being who is the eternal, self-existing, sovereign, holy creator!

YHWH is the name by which God chooses to be known.[4] There can be only one God who is distinguished from all the false gods because he alone is the holy, self-existing, eternal, sovereign Creator of all things.

## We Worship God by Faith

We Christians worship the God of the Bible, revealed in Jesus Christ, as the true God, but we can worship this true God only by faith. Only by faith are we enabled to reach beyond the visible created world in which we live and to encounter the true God in the only place we can find him, in the unseen world outside our created world. The words *by faith* recur twenty-one times in Hebrews 11. We are told not only what a "great cloud" of witnesses did by faith, but how faith is the basis for the right worship of the right God.

> Now faith is being sure of what we hope for and certain of what we do not see. This is what the ancients were commended for.
>
> By faith we understand that the universe was formed at God's command, so that what is seen was not made out of what was visible. . . . And without faith it is impossible to please God, because anyone who comes to him must believe that he exists and that he rewards those who earnestly seek him. [Heb. 11:1–3, 6]

From the outset, the worship of God is a matter of faith. We are born into a physical world, a world of senses by which we see, touch, taste, smell, and hear. Because we were created to live in a sensory world, a time-space box, it is natural—in the purest sense of the word—for us to conclude that the physical world is the ultimate reality because it is so immediate. The physical world so plays on our senses that we can easily become insensitive to the nonphysical world that is not only real, but the highest reality. It is the higher reality because "what is seen was not made out of what was visible."

Yet the clues are there for us to discern an immaterial and unseen reality that coexists with, yet transcends, immediate material reality. We begin to realize that immaterial qualities such as love, truth, justice, and hope cannot be housed in a strictly material world. How we realize that is difficult to describe; our immaterial senses cannot be analyzed in the terms we use to describe our physical senses. Yet Ecclesiastes tells us that God has "placed eternity in the hearts of men"— the capacity to perceive that this temporal and finite physical world is not the highest reality. Don Richardson documented that this immaterial sixth sense has been the key to finding God for peoples and tribes scattered in even the most remote places on earth.[5] The journey toward the true God begins with this realization: there is an unseen reality that is as certain as the material reality that surrounds us.

By faith—a nonmaterial sixth sense—we are able to perceive the unseen reality, a spiritual world where God rules and from which he created all things, including the physical. By faith we "see" beyond the creation to the Creator. By faith we "look" beyond the false gods fashioned out of the material world and see the true God. By faith we "hear" God speak to us from outside our world of sound waves. By faith we "taste" and see that he is good.

So, says the author of Hebrews, to approach the true God, we must believe that he exists, albeit in a higher unseen reality, and that it is worth our effort to look outside our material world to find him in that higher unseen reality.

## The Reward for Worship

Our discussion of worshiping God by faith brings us almost naturally to the question of the motivation and the benefits of worship. The truth that God rewards "those who earnestly seek him" brings us back to the question with which we began this chapter: Why do we worship God? Do we worship God for who he is? Clearly the Word of God gives us ample reason to worship God: He is our holy, eternal, sovereign Creator! He has commanded us to worship him rather than the false gods. We have sufficient cause to worship him.

Or do we worship God only for a reward?

As we observed earlier, the marketing of church has led to dangerous application of church growth principles to the "now" generation that demands instant gratification or at least instant feedback. A marketing orientation only serves to validate instant gratification as a reasonable attribute of worship. As Hebrews 11 points out clearly, the ancients were willing to worship and serve God for an eternal reward. That is a concept foreign to the modern mind.

The problems caused by this emphasis leak out all over. Scottish churchman and American church-watcher Alistair Begg warns, "We are drifting toward a religion which consciously or unconsciously has its eye on humanity rather than on deity."[6]

When a whole generation fails to grasp the truth that the real reward for those who seek God diligently is to find God himself, the result is self-centered religion. In one of the first statements God made to Abram, God declared "I am your great reward" (Gen. 15:1). We must see the subtle difference between "you will seek me and find me" and "you will seek me and find a reward." God, not his reward, are the reason for worship. We worship God not for tangible reward, whether satisfaction or prosperity. God himself is our reward.

# WORSHIPING GOD THE RIGHT WAY

We who worship the true, living God
would be better if not completely different if we worshiped him better. For to
worship him as we ought is to become
what we ought.
—Ben Patterson,
*Christianity Today*

## Confusion in the Ranks

It was the first Sunday of the summer at a fairly typical
evangelical church not far from my home in the Los Angeles area. The senior pastor had arranged to have a worship
team lead the service to put a "spark" into the otherwise
depressed summer vacation season. The worship team
moved the pulpit aside, rolled the baby grand piano to the
center of the large platform, plugged in an electronic key-
board, and focused their overhead projector. As the service
began, the words of choruses (complete with CCLI infor-
mation, of course) were projected on the screen. Some songs
were new to the congregation, some better known. The service was less formal than that of Sundays past, but the music

barely approached one-tenth the volume of a Michael W. Smith concert—no drums, no ten-foot-high speaker columns.

Many worshipers seemed to enjoy the new format. Others remained politely stoic. Little could the pastor have anticipated the size of the blast his "spark" would ignite. It would come to be measured in megatons.

Following the service, several members of the congregation stormed the platform to denounce the "debauchery" to which they had been reluctant witnesses. Sound-system operators threw down their keys and walked out in protest. One saint spat on the floor in disgust and threatened never to return. The church was thrown into turmoil. The explosion started a series of California-style brush fires that have yet to be "knocked down."

In the next three months people left, the pastor came under vicious personal attack for petty issues (everything from owning a pick-up truck to wearing brightly colored slacks to a church picnic) and was soon forced to resign. The music director was gone. The worship team had moved on. Several months later litigation was initiated to prevent any further incursion of contemporary worship into the church. What began as an attempt by a pastor to offer acceptable worship to God continued for more than a year to tear apart the body of Christ and to dishonor God—even before the pagans.

Not everyone, it appears, agrees as to what it means to worship the right God in the right way!

The incident at this church in my neighborhood—not Mr. Rogers' neighborhood, to be sure—may be sad and ugly, but it is certainly not isolated. The styles in question may be different or even the reverse of those I related, but thousands of churches in the United States are at some point along the continuum between debate and destruction over the issue of what is the right kind of worship to offer God. The debate has become not only as intense and divisive as is the pro-choice/pro-life debate in the American political arena, but it also seems to have become too often an emotional debate that ignores the available biblical instruction. The need for instruction in how to worship properly appears to be constant. We cannot expect that God's people in each generation will intuitively know what it means to worship God in the right way. It is not enough to simply pass on our traditional practices of worship. Isolated pockets of snake handlers remind us that traditions can lead us astray.

In every generation the church must look beyond traditions and seek instruction from God's Word: What does it mean in this generation to worship God in the right way? As we have already noted, the Bible warns against false worship (worship of the wrong God; Exod. 20:3–5; Isa. 44:6–17; 46:5–9) but it also warns against vain worship (worship of the right God in the wrong way; Amos 5:21–22; Mark 7:6–8).

How many me-generation evangelicals are in search of a church that will provide them with a high degree of satisfaction from the worship service? Satisfaction may be nebulously defined as "receiving a blessing," "getting pumped up," "being fed," or "feeling the Spirit move." It may be measured more specifically in terms of "excitement" or even of being "slain in the Spirit." In each case the emphasis is on the satisfaction of the worshiper and how the worship experience made him or her feel.

And how many now-generation evangelicals have been misled into assuming that since we have not been formally notified to the contrary, our self-centered worship must be acceptable to God? We do not have God's feedback to continually monitor God's level of satisfaction with our worship and remind us that his pleasure is our primary purpose. The only feedback concerning our worship is related to the level of satisfaction that worshipers experience.

Of course, God regularly grades our worship, but report cards will not be given out until graduation. How different would our worship be if the instant-gratification generation could receive instant feedback on its worship?

I wonder what might happen if report cards were given to worshipers each Sunday. They could be like my daughter's first-grade report card: "O" for outstanding, "S" for satisfactory, "N" for needs improvement, and "U" for unacceptable. We can debate whether people would get a zero for those Sundays they decided they could worship God just as well at the beach or the church of the innersprings—but those would have to be mailed. In the spirit of first grade, we could keep the categories simple.

### Illustration 3.1
*Worship Report Card*

| | | | | |
|---|---|---|---|---|
| Preparation and punctuality | O | S | N | U |
| Singing offered to God | O | S | N | U |
| Other offerings of praise | O | S | N | U |
| Joined in prayer | O | S | N | U |
| Gifts and offerings given | O | S | N | U |
| Listened to God | O | S | N | U |
| Internalized the message | O | S | N | U |
| Attitude | O | S | N | U |
| Spirit/truth balanced | O | S | N | U |

It might sound like a good idea until we remember what happened the last time the sovereign holy God gave out immediate report cards: Ananias and Sapphira died and were carried away to be buried (Acts 5).

Since actual report cards will not be distributed until graduation (1 Cor. 3:13), perhaps in the interim it might be worth our while to invest in some serious self-evaluation. Hebrews 10:24–25 seems to suggest some sort of mutual accountability as we are exhorted to "spur one another on toward love and good deeds," and to make sure we not "give up meeting together, as some are in the habit of doing, but let us encourage one another."

There is an urgent need for a corrective to widespread human-centered worship. The degree to which this rampant existentialism has affected our culture was exposed recently by former Secretary of Education William Bennett in an interview on public television. When the interviewer asked why Japanese students perform so much better than American students in math, Bennett said tersely: "Japanese students go to math class and talk about math. American students go to math class and talk about how they feel about math."

To paraphrase Bennett: We used to go to church to worship; now we go to church and talk about how we feel about worship.

The existentialism of our contemporary culture has flooded the church and is spilling out all over. Our focus on how satisfied we feel about worship rather than on the quality of our offering to God may be the most obvious manifestation. Michael Wiebe wrote: "Disappointment because of the absence of a particular feeling reveals an attitude bordering on idolatry. Seeking and experience in worship elevates man above God; it diverts our attention from his majesty to our internal response."[1] I have sought here to refocus our eyes on the right reasons for worshiping God the right God. Having reaffirmed the God of the Bible as the right God, worthy of worship, we need to ask what is the right way to worship him. It is important because we will be different if we worship him better.

## The Precedent for Right Worship

God called Israel to be a people to worship him and to make his name known among all the nations of the earth.

In Exodus 5:1, 3, we read of God's call to Hebrew slaves in Egypt, a call to come and worship:

> Afterward, Moses and Aaron went to Pharaoh and said, "This is what the LORD, the God of Israel says: 'Let my people go, so that they may hold a festival to me in the desert'" . . .
> Then they said, "The God of the Hebrews has met with us. Now let us take a three-day journey into the desert to offer sacrifices to the LORD our God . . ."

In the initial call to the Hebrews (Exod. 4:29–6:12) we discover three important principles of right worship. These principles are simple, even obvious, but they establish a foundation for us.

First, right worship revolves around the name of YHWH, the God of the Hebrews. Moses had spoken to Pharaoh with devastating results as Pharaoh imposed his infamous edict (Exod. 5:6–9). Moses argued with God that speaking to Pharaoh "in [God's] name" had "brought trouble upon this people."

God made it clear to Moses that his name was at issue. He would deliver the people of Israel from Egypt not by the eloquence of men, nor by the kindness of Pharaoh, but by the undeniable power of God. To make sure that YHWH would be glorified by the exodus, it was necessary to harden Pharaoh's heart: "I will take you as my own people, and I will be your God. Then you will know that I am the LORD (YHWH) your God who brought you out from under the yoke of the Egyptians" (6:7).

Second, right worship of God also reacts to his character. When Moses first appeared to the leaders of Israel, he declared to them the caring character of the God of their fathers:

> Moses and Aaron brought together all the elders of the Israelites, and Aaron told them everything the LORD had said

to Moses. He also performed the signs before the people, and they believed. And when they heard that the LORD was concerned about them and had seen their misery, they bowed down and worshiped. [4:29–31]

They responded to a revelation of God's character with worship, believing that God cared about them and that God had sufficient power to do something about their misery. Right worship is based on a revealed knowledge of God's character. It appears that the two qualities of love (care) and power are significant to many potential worshipers. For many people today, human suffering is a major obstacle to worshiping God because the modern mind often sees suffering as reason to question the love of God, the power of God, or both.

Suffering generates a common argument about God: "Either he doesn't care about the suffering, or he is powerless to do anything about the suffering." Shelves have been cluttered with books arguing that God is not powerful enough to intervene in human suffering. The Holocaust has become the focal point in this debate for many Jews, including Rabbi Harold Kushner who argues that God is simply not able to suppress evil and the suffering it brings.[2]

We see that ancient Israel struggled with the same issue. When Pharaoh punished the Hebrews, significantly increasing their workload, they ceased to worship YHWH, doubting his care and his power to deliver them from their suffering. God told Moses that this was all part of his plan for his glory. The people of Israel were not convinced: "Moses reported this to the Israelites, but they did not listen to him because of their discouragement and cruel bondage" (6:9). How much we are like them. We are reminded that our worship is built on the same foundation—believing that God cares and is powerful.

We are frequently confronted by the problem of suffering. On a recent flight to Tel Aviv, I engaged in a long conversation with an American Jewish woman, Hilda, who displayed a broad understanding of religions. Our pleasant conversation took an abrupt shift when she told me that God died for her when her parents died in Auschwitz. There can be no God, she argued, and the Holocaust is her evidence. Her conclusion is, of course, existential: God failed her, therefore God died. God either didn't care or didn't have the power to stop the Holocaust. In either case, he is not a God she can bother with.

Having previously visited several of the death camps, I think I was able to be genuinely sympathetic to her. I then told her a story of Chuck Schwarz, a friend and associate of mine who is a missionary in Russia. In 1982 Chuck lost both of his parents when a drunk driver killed them. The driver, Ellis, was arrested and convicted of vehicular manslaughter and was entenced to two years in the New York state prison at Jamesville. A chaplain's intervention and an exchange of letters led Chuck and his wife to make a number of visits to the prison. The Schwarzes offered the young man forgiveness based on the grace of Jesus Christ. Ellis came to believe in Jesus Christ while in prison, finished his term, and now ministers and preaches at the prison. Suffering, it seems, causes the existentialist to abandon God, but the same suffering causes others to embrace him.[3]

Hilda listened politely and then dismissed the story—not because she didn't believe it, but because she maintained that her loss of both parents in Auschwitz was a far greater loss and resulted in far greater suffering than Chuck's loss of both parents in an alcohol-related auto accident. The truth of the Schwarz case did not apply to her.

The problem of suffering has turned many away from God. We worship God because we believe he is loving and because he is able to care for his own. It is not a surprise that suffering attacks and tests our worship of God at a foundational level.

Third, true worship requires sacrifice. It is dangerous in our era of self-centered Christianity to mention the word *sacrifice*. Worship does involve sacrifice. It must. If we think of worship as those acts that ascribe worth to God, then we must offer to him something of worth to us. This is not onerous, however, for Moses speaks to Pharaoh of this ministry to God as both a "festival" and a "sacrifice." A three-day trip into the horrendous wilderness of Sinai was no vacation— even from bondage in Egypt.

Sacrifice can be as simple as taking an hour each week to offer genuine praise to God (Heb. 13:15). However, it is increasingly obvious that professing believers in America are less and less willing to sacrifice the time for worship. We should be concerned but not alarmed. Futurists argue that time, not money, is the real treasure of the 1990s. We can observe a growing pattern of worship among many who claim to be Christians—go early and get out early. The motive seems to be to preserve most of the Lord's day for ourselves and to offer to God our less valuable time slots.

The basic principles of right worship must be continually reinforced. Forty years after Moses first spoke to Pharaoh on behalf of God's people, Moses instructed them concerning proper worship: "You must not worship the LORD your God in their way, because in worshiping their gods, they do all kinds of detestable things the LORD hates. They even burn their sons and daughters in the fire as sacrifices to their gods" (Deut. 12:31). The people of God were moving into the land of Canaan, where pagan worship, especially that of the various Baal gods, threatened to influence the nation of Israel. The people had already crafted one golden calf and engaged in a night of offensive idolatry. The temptation for them to take instruction in worship from others rather than YHWH was still there forty years later.

## The Basic Qualities of Right Worship

The most important foundational teaching in the New Testament comes from an unlikely source: Jesus' conversation with the Samaritan woman at the well. The woman inquired of Jesus: Who worshiped God the right way, the Jews in Jerusalem or the Samaritans at Gerazim? His answer is concise and instructive:

> "Believe me, woman, a time is coming when you will worship the Father neither on this mountain nor in Jerusalem. You Samaritans worship what you do not know; we worship what we do know, for salvation is from the Jews. Yet a time is coming and has now come when the true worshipers will worship the Father in spirit and truth, for they are the kind of worshipers the Father seeks. God is spirit, and his worshipers must worship in spirit and in truth." [John 4:21–24]

One of the keys to understanding this passage comes from two phrases, similar yet curiously different. In verse 21 Jesus says that "a time is coming." In verse 23 Jesus says that "a time is coming and has now come." These two phrases are the passageways into the first two of the three principles.

In the first instance Jesus spoke of the time when the temple of God would no longer be a building in Jerusalem, for it would be destroyed. The temple would be established by the coming Holy Spirit in the heart of each beliver. So, Jesus first revealed that while certain settings may be more conducive to worship than others, worship is dependent upon a place no longer.

Yes, the church needs a place to meet; but the need for expensive cathedrals (or sanctuaries or worship centers) is often questionable. I have in mind especially some of the single-purpose auditoriums with fixed seats, sloped floors, projection television screens, and fifteen-million-dollar price tags. We can rationalize today's worship centers by appealing to the prototype in Jerusalem and to the prophet Haggai, who endorsed a temple worthy of God, but the analogy is not compelling. There was only one temple for the nation and many synagogues of a much more humble and practical nature. Moreover, the temple existed to provide a place for bloody animal sacrifice, a flaming altar, and a secure and inaccessible dwelling for the shekinah glory of God behind the veil.

Many churches—not just those with fifteen-million-dollar buildings—are building-bound, building-driven and building-oriented. A building-oriented church is one whose ministry is either dominated by or severely limited by its building costs. The building-oriented church is continually tempted to become human-centered to pay for its building. The scenario is this:

> the church calls or discovers a dynamic preacher
> the church begins to attract people, many from other churches
> the church outgrows its facilities (as utilized)
> the new building is needed because other people want to hear the dynamic preacher
> the big building is built for all the people who will come
> the people who came now become needed so they can help to pay for the building

The dynamic preacher has a terrible burden: he must hold on to his audience at any cost so they can pay for the building. In our trend-conscious evangelical world, where church loyalty is as common as a rotary phone, "retaining market share" of baby boomers is not easy. In the land of the megachurch, when large churches lose people to other large churches, the empty seats are counted in the hundreds. The stakes are high to keep those "revenue-producing seats" filled.[4] Megachurch pastor Kenneth Chapin admitted,

"Growth is the bottom line of a superchurch, and this puts enormous pressure on the church to measure itself with a different measuring stick than God has."[5]

In such an environment, the building-oriented church can be tempted to shift its focus from reaching the community and proclaiming the gospel to filling the seats and keeping the donors happy. The building-oriented church runs the danger of shifting from being a market-sensitive church to being a consumer-driven church where worship becomes human-centered and the prophetic voice of the church is silenced by an intimidating mortgage. In the building-oriented church it is easy to forget that the goal of the church is to equip and send the saints into the world, not to see how many people can be attracted to a meeting on Sunday morning.

The problem is as old as the temple in Jerusalem. Jesus had to be sacrificed, the high priest declared, because what he was saying was not popular and the Romans might "take away our place" (the temple). It is little wonder Jesus began by severing worship from a place. Israel was dominated by its place of worship rather than its object of worship. The temple had become a capital intensive enterprise, a monster that needed to be fed.

Jesus then says that "a time is coming and has now come when the true worshipers will worship the Father in spirit and truth" (4:23). Here Jesus contrasted the worship of the Samaritans at Mount Gerazim in Samaria with the worship of the Jews at Mount Zion in Jerusalem. The Samaritans, Jesus pointed out, worshiped ignorantly (v. 22). They lacked needed truth and knowledge of the One whom they were worshiping. Although the worship at Gerazim was unacceptable because of the Samaritans' ignorance, it was nonetheless enthusiastic, active, and fervent.

Down the road in Jerusalem the Jews worshiped God with much more knowledge if not understanding. The Jews were a nation of career priests, of meticulous scholars, and of theologically obsessed Pharisees. They did not lack knowledge about God or how to worship, but they were without enthusiasm. Their worship constituted dead orthodoxy.

The worshiper that God desires worships in both spirit and truth. Jesus instructed us that right worship must include both heartfelt involvement and sound knowledge— it engages both left brain and right brain. Worship in spirit engages the whole being: our minds, our senses, and our feelings. Worship in truth engages our mind, our intellect, and our reasoning. Proper worship is cognitive and objective, but it also embraces the abstract, the artistic, and the subjective part of our lives. The Lord's call to worship in spirit and truth recognizes that we are whole people with two distinct capacities.

The third important principle Jesus taught is that worship (salvation) is from the Jews. Because salvation is from the Jews, it is logical that instruction about worship begins from the Jews as well. The starting place for instruction in worship is the Old Testament. While the Old Testament is full of "types and shadows" and is not always easy to apply to worship in the church age, it is a vast storehouse of instruction on worship.

Psalm 145:1–13 provides but one solid Old Testament example of instruction about worship:

I will *exalt* you, my *God the King*;
    I will *praise your name* for ever and ever.
Every day I will *praise* you
    and *extol* your name for ever and ever.

*Great is the* Lord and most worthy of praise;
    his *greatness no one can fathom.*
One generation will *commend* your *works* to another;
    they will *tell* of your *mighty acts.*
They will *speak of the glorious splendor* of your *majesty,*
    and I will *meditate* on your *wonderful works.*

They will *tell* of the power of your *awesome works*,
and I will **proclaim** your *great deeds*.
They will **celebrate** your abundant *goodness*
and **joyfully sing** of your *righteousness*.

The LORD is *gracious and compassionate,*
*slow to anger* and *rich in love.*
The LORD is *good* to all;
he *has compassion* on *all he has made.*
All you have made will **praise** you, O LORD;
your saints will **extol** you.
They will **tell** of the *glory* of your kingdom
and **speak** of your *might,*
so that all men may know of your *mighty acts*
and the *glorious splendor* of your kingdom.
Your kingdom is an *everlasting* kingdom,
and your *dominion endures* through all generations.

In these few verses is a full lexicon of worship. The many reasons for worshiping God are articulated (in italics): his good character, his great deeds, and for being God. The psalmist employs a rich menu of expression for how God is to be worshiped (in boldface italics): extol, praise, proclaim.

This Hebrew manual of worship provides a treasure of instruction on worship. There are songs to sing and new songs to learn. There are prayers of confession, adoration, petition and even imprecation. There are instructions to worship God with raised hands, with dancing, on bended knees, with shouting, with clapping, by continual repetition of single phrases, and even by anointing with oil. There are exhortations to worship God with a range of feelings: reverence, awe, joy, fear, gladness, celebration, humility, and contrition. There are suggestions to employ in our worship instruments from all groups: brass, strings, woodwinds, and percussion (Ps. 150). There is, in fact, such a diversity of expression of worship as to incorporate almost anything that the sanctified heart might imagine. The Old Testament teaches us that when it comes to worshiping the God of heaven, the sky is the limit!

The psalms supply us with a lexicon of terms to embrace our activities that glorify God: exalt, adore, praise. A brief look at just three expressions of worship helps us see the nuances that serve to guide us as worshipers (illustration 3.2).

Worship involves many different expressions. It is hard to imagine that with Psalms as our instruction book we could be led to worship that is dull, predictable, and routine. Such is the heritage and the legacy of the Jews to us as worshipers.

## Defining Worship

A working definition of worship may serve us well at this point. While there are many, I offer one I adapted from a mentor who first opened my eyes to the nature of true worship.

> Worship is
> active communion with God
> in which believers by grace
> and through faith
> focus their hearts' affection
> and minds' attention
> on humbly glorifying God
> in response to his character,
> his acts,
> and his Word.[6]

A good working definition of worship helps us to focus on what is essential for worship, what is secondary, and what is irrelevant. Worship is a reactive process, a dialogue between God and humans in which God is always the initiator. He impresses us with his character and his acts;

## Illustration 3:2
### *The Expressions of Worship**

| Adoration | Thanksgiving | Praise |
|---|---|---|
| Contemplative worship, which focuses on the beauty and splendor of God to delight in his character | Grateful worship in which believers respond with expressions of joyful and humble appreciation to the gifts, the favor, the blessings, and the specific actions of God | Celebrative worship in which believers glorify and exalt God through enthusiastic and uninhibited expression of rejoicing in God's names, acts, and character |
| **Addressed** to God | **Addressed** to God | **Addressed** to God |
| **Focus** Person of God | **Focus** Works of God | **Focus** Person and works of God |
| **Spirit** Reflective | **Spirit** Appreciative | **Spirit** Celebrative |
| **Dynamic** Intimate | **Dynamic** Corporate | **Dynamic** Corporate |

* Bruce Leafblad, untitled lecture on worship (San Diego: Bethel Theological Seminary, West Campus, January 1985).

we respond in a wide range of appropriate expressions that glorify God.

In Isaiah 6:1–8, a drama unfolds that gives us a model of worship in spirit and truth as God intended:

In the year that King Uzziah died, I saw the Lord seated
on a throne, high and exalted, and the train of his robe filled
the temple. Above him were seraphs, each with six wings:
With two wings they covered their faces, with two they covered their feet, and with two they were flying. And they were
calling to one another:

> Holy, holy, holy is the LORD Almighty;
> the whole earth is full of his glory.

At the sound of their voices the doorposts and thresholds
shook and the temple was filled with smoke.
"Woe to me!" I cried. "I am ruined! For I am a man of
unclean lips, and I live among a people of unclean lips, and
my eyes have seen the King, the LORD Almighty."
Then one of the seraphs flew to me with a live coal in his
hand, which he had taken with tongs from the altar. With it
he touched my mouth and said, "See, this has touched your
lips; your guilt is taken away and your sin atoned for."
Then I heard the voice of the Lord saying, "Whom shall
I send? And who will go for us?"
And I said, "Here am I. Send me!"

A distinctive and instructive pattern emerges from this
drama.

### Illustration 3.3
#### *The Drama of Worship*

| | |
|---|---|
| Revelation of God | Isaiah sees God |
| Adoration and praise | Angels worship God |
| Conviction | God's holiness convicts Isaiah |
| Confession | Isaiah acknowledges sin |
| Expiation | God takes away Isaiah's sin |
| Proclamation | Sermon: "Who Will Go?" |
| Dedication | Isaiah commits himself anew |

We must not miss the thread: Isaiah confessed the sin of unclean lips; God cleansed Isaiah's unclean lips; God sent Isaiah, now cleansed, to go and proclaim God's Word with his lips.

The drama is reactive, a series of impressive events that trigger a series of responsive expressions of worship (illustration 3.4). By seeing Isaiah 6:1–8 as a drama we gain a valuable basic insight into worship.

### Illustration 3.4
#### *The Dialogue of Worship*

God impresses us:

We respond to God:

| God impresses us: | We respond to God: |
|---|---|
| God reveals himself seated on the throne. | |
| | The angels glorify God: "Holy, Holy, Holy!" |
| The glory of God shakes the foundation of the temple. | |
| | Isaiah recognizes and confesses his sin: "Woe to me." |
| The angel touches Isaiah's lips with a coal and declares that his sin and guilt have been removed. | |
| | Isaiah is transformed in the presence of God. |
| The Word of God is proclaimed: "Who will go for us?" | |
| | Isaiah commits himself to serving God: "Here am I. Send me!" |

It may well have been Søren Kierkegaard who first taught a dramatic view of worship in which God is the audience, the congregation is the cast of actors and, according to most of his students, the leaders are the directors (others refine Kierkegaard's view and see the Holy Spirit as the director). In any case, worship is not a spectator sport! True worship is hard work offered to God sacrificially by worshipers who understand that God is the consumer of the worship as well as its sponsor. Worship is for God's pleasure and benefit.

The dramatic view is important because it argues against the worshiper-as-spectator orientation that is so pronounced in our culture. The worshiper-as-spectator view sees worship primarily as entertainment to enjoy, critique, and evaluate. The consumer of worship is not God, but the so-called worshiper. The distinction that comes from the dramatic view is elementary but crucial. When the distinction is blurred, the whole purpose of the church is in danger of coming under the unbiblical influences of our contemporary and consumer-oriented culture.

Yet, because so many have failed to notice the distinction and others have failed to maintain the distinction between God the consumer and the worshiper as consumer that the seemingly self-evident question "Whom is worship for?" must be asked. We are navigating in an age of human-centered Christianity and warnings like Alistair Begg's (chap. 2) must be sounded.

The drama in Isaiah is inspiring and instructive, but we can question whether it should serve to establish a fixed pattern for worship, such as the Catholic mass:

Kyrie
Gloria
Credo
Sanctus
Agnus Dei

The New Testament reveals no set formula for worship. In Jerusalem, worship was rooted in the temple; the church worshiped there for some time before moving into homes (Acts 2:46). In Antioch, worship was influenced by Hellenistic Jews who were the core of the church (Acts 11:20). They began to worship in the synagogue according to the patterns of the synagogue (praise, prayer, and proclamation). In Corinth the church had few members with Jewish roots, as converts came primarily from paganism. Worship in Corinth was so nearly without structure that Paul gave the congregation some guidelines to make sure things were decent and orderly (1 Cor. 14). We see some structure in the worship of the first-century church, but no pattern or formula for worship is prescribed in the New Testament. Worship differed in Jerusalem and Antioch and Corinth. We can argue, then, that there is almost no limit to the variety of expressions of worship that sanctified believers can creatively adapt and employ to honor our great God.

## Right Worship Modeled for Us

While worship at Mount Zion lacked enthusiasm and worship at Mount Gerazim lacked understanding, worship on the Mount of Olives, in the village of Bethany, models a splendid balance. John records some of the details of a worship service that differs from any other, yet embodies spirit and truth.

Six days before the Passover, Jesus arrived at Bethany, where Lazarus lived, whom Jesus had raised from the dead. Here a dinner was given in Jesus' honor. Martha served, while Lazarus was among those reclining at the table with him. Then Mary took about a pint of pure nard, an expensive perfume; she poured it on Jesus' feet and wiped his feet with her hair. And the house was filled with the fragrance of the perfume. But one of his disciples, Judas Iscariot, who was

later to betray him, objected, "Why wasn't this perfume sold
and the money given to the poor? It was worth a year's wages."
He did not say this because he cared about the poor but
because he was a thief; as keeper of the money bag, he used
to help himself to what was put into it. [12:1–6]

Although it is clearly outside the bounds of traditional
worship, a dinner given in Jesus' honor certainly qualifies as
an appropriate expression of worship. In fact, the pericope
provides some remarkable instruction on the nature of true
worship.

Lazarus, the sponsor, had recently been brought from
death to life and had a heart overflowing with praise for
Jesus. His sisters also were worshipers pleased with the
opportunity not only to reverence Jesus, but also to serve
him.

There were many preparations to make for the dinner;
but Martha, in harmony with her sister, was focused on the
goal of honoring Jesus and not just entertaining various
guests.

Mary, one who had already learned to be at home at Jesus'
feet, served as the leader of worship. She took a vial of perfume (worth a year's wage, or perhaps twenty thousand dollars today) and anointed Jesus' feet as an act of love and worship. The sponsor, Lazarus, must have given his hearty
consent to such an elaborate expression of worship. This
was a deeply felt act of love and honor.

It seems likely that the perfume was purchased specifically for this event. If Lazarus had kept in his home jars of
perfume suitable for preserving a body, it seems logical that
they would have been emptied in preparing Lazarus's own
body when he was buried just a few days before. Nonetheless, it is a most appropriate offering in light of who gave it
and who received it: Jesus noted that the perfume was a fitting offering for him because it prepared his body for bur-
ial. This memorable act of worship transformed the home

into a sanctuary for worship as the fragrance of the perfume filled the house.

Not everyone present in the sanctuary at Bethany was worshiping. Judas was not! It takes more than being in a sanctuary where others are worshiping to be a worshiper. Judas—for dishonest reasons and sounding very much like a Pharisee—protested that the money should not have been used to anoint Jesus but should have been given to the poor. Judas could attend a dinner in Jesus' honor without betraying the content of his heart. But Judas became uncomfortable when others began to worship Jesus; Judas could not and would not add his worship or his "amen" to theirs. His heart was exposed. In essence, Judas was declaring that while Jesus may have been worthy of a testimonial dinner, he was not worthy of sacrificial expressions of worship such as the one Mary offered to him.

Jesus, on the other hand, received the worship and commended the worshiper. In doing so, Jesus reminded the people that no offering or expression of worship is too great to honor him! This worship service in Bethany in many ways epitomizes worship of the right God in the right way!

*Worship is not dependent upon an elaborate building.* A home in Bethany was sanctified by its owner.

*Worship is clearly purposeful.* Fellowship and food were enjoyed at Bethany, but the singular purpose was to honor the One worthy of honor. When the house filled with the fragrance, everyone was reminded again of the purpose for the dinner.

*Creative worship may employ new and meaningful ways to worship* with enthusiasm (in spirit) that are consistent with God's Word (in truth). God is the creator of vast diversity. Our worship of him should rightly reflect a measure of that creativity and diversity. It is beyond the purview of Scripture to mandate an order of worship (liturgical to spontaneous) or a style of worship (contemporary to traditional). There are only a few guidelines and no prescription for worship for those seeking to devise the perfect order of worship for next Sunday. We are left to the leading of the Holy Spirit within the boundaries established by Jesus: in spirit and in truth.

*Worship must be active and engaging.* Passive worship is an oxymoron. Judas was not transformed into a worshiper by being in the house filled with the fragrance of others' offerings. Neither are spectators on Sunday mornings transformed into worshipers by sitting in the soft light filtered through stained glass. We may be pleased that people are present in our churches—it is better that they be there than washing the car. But let us not pretend that they are all worshipers because of their presence. They are still spectators.

*No expression of worship is too great to offer to Jesus.* As we grow as worshipers we discover the only limits to our worship are our own internal limits on our love, our generosity, or our sense of self-consciousness.

*Self-consciousness is the great enemy of worship.* Obviously, Mary did not concern herself with what others might think or say about her conspicuous expression of worship. Her focus was on her Lord as she knelt at his feet. Judas felt uncomfortable with her act of worship.

Some Christians today who attend noncharismatic churches would like to raise their hands in demonstrative worship. They are often made to feel self-conscious or even unspiritual by the formal or informal network that tells them: "That's not done here." One music director confessed to me that he was gently censured for momentarily closing his eyes during a reflective worship song. Conversely, there are worshipers in charismatic churches who are made to feel self-conscious or unspiritual if they don't raise their hands or don't dance or are not slain in the Spirit. In both cases, self-consciousness is the enemy of true worship.

Worship "in spirit and truth" gives us permission *to appreciate and employ a wide range of worship expressions* within the body of Christ without feeling obligated to express our worship in any particular way!

## Right Worship Is Seeker-Sensitive

Having warned against the dangers of the church growth movement, it may seem contradictory for me to suggest that true worship is seeker-sensitive. It is fitting that the corporate act of worship should attract others to become worshipers of God.

Although Paul never used the term *seeker-sensitive,* I would argue that he pioneered the concept. Paul acknowledged that the gospel itself is a stumbling block to many, especially the Jews, and he was much concerned that the church not put any manmade stumbling blocks along the path of an unbeliever moving toward God (2 Cor. 6:3). In 1 Corinthians 10 Paul addressed the subject of meat offered to idols. If an unbeliever invites you to a meal, writes Paul, don't make an issue of where the meat came from. Because an idol is not real, a Christian is free to eat meat offered to an idol—so long as the Christian did not participate. Don't make the issue of the meat a stumbling block to an unbeliever; use your freedom to advance the gospel. Our evangelical house rules may be important to us, but they can be obstacles to unbelievers.

In his clearest statement, Paul writes in his first letter to Corinth that worship in the church should be seeker-sensitive. Because Paul's instruction was in response to specific problems in the church, it does not appear that he intended his instruction to be either exhaustive or systematic. Instead, we can glean several strong suggestions Paul makes in chapters 11 and 14:

> dress and appearance should not be offensive (11:2–16)
> dissension or disunity must be kept out of the church (11:17–19)

the Lord's Supper should be eaten in a worthy manner—
no drunks or gluttons, please (11:20–34)
prophetic teaching is essential but must be orderly
(14:39, 22–25, 29–32)
tongues must be carefully integrated (14:1–19, 27–28)
everyone should be encouraged to participate actively
(14:26, 34–38)

All of this instruction serves to guide the church in worship
that will insure that believers are truly free to worship with
enthusiasm but with concern for "an unbeliever or someone
who does not understand" (14:24). Paul summarizes his
balanced instruction in the last verse of chapter 14: "But
everything should be done in a fitting and orderly way."
Right worship, argues Paul, is inherently compelling, even
to unbelievers. When people actively approach God in fresh,
creative, and joyful worship, others will be drawn to God's
alien beauty. While Paul seeks to insure that the church in
Corinth remains sensitive to the unbeliever, being sensitive
to the presence of non-Christians does not require compromising the integrity (truth) of worship or compromising
the prophetic message for the sake of reaching the non-
Christian who is present:

> [I]f . . . an unbeliever or someone who does not understand
> comes in while everybody is prophesying, he will be con-
> vinced by all that he is a sinner and will be judged by all, and
> the secrets of his heart will be laid bare. So he will fall down
> and worship God, exclaiming, "God is really among you."
> [14:24–25]

Examination of the context is revealing. The ministry of
prophecy in the church will convict unbelievers of sin and
convert them to worshipers of God. So Paul advocates that
worship should include "a word of instruction, a revelation"
(v. 26), that two or three prophets should speak, and that

others should weigh carefully what the prophets say. Although some scholars see this passage as dealing with "prophecies," Wayne Grudem builds a strong case for us to see the "prophet" here as the preacher/teacher who is simply preaching/teaching the Word of God to the church.[7]

For the church to be seeker-sensitive is right and proper, but being seeker-sensitive does not extend to the content of our preaching! Paul encouraged the church to make sure worship services were not repelling unbelievers because the services were chaotic, disorderly, or marked by disunity. But the Word of God is not to be tampered with in the name of making our services seeker-sensitive! There is no suggestion from God's Word that prophets should proclaim a more sensitive message, a message that humans have merely not lived up to their potential—a message that avoids making unbelievers feel "convinced by all" that they are sinners. Nor is there instruction to preach only the inclusive message of God's love so that unbelievers will be able to stand tall before God by faith rather than fall down before him and say, "God is really among you." Quite the contrary!

Yet, as we will see in the following two chapters, seeker sensitivity has led some preachers to abandon their prophetic role in the church and to preach something other than the good news that God saves sinners by grace.

PART **2**

# THE ROLE
# OF GRACE
# IN THE CHRISTIAN LIFE

# GRACE: THE PROPER BASIS OF WORSHIP

Amazing grace! how sweet the sound,
That saved a wretch like me!
I once was lost, but now am found,
Was blind, but now I see.

—John Newton

## Poles Apart from God

My son has a toddler-sized, wooden train set that continually frustrates him. He cannot manage to couple the magnetically joined cars. After all, he perceives that the magnets front and back look alike and reveal no clues as to how they should be coupled or why they defy being coupled. When he does not have the poles lined up properly, north to south, the cars not only will not link together, but repel each other. Were not the magnets made to be coupled together? His young mind cannot understand the unseen force that causes two similar poles to repel each other.

Any schoolchild knows that two magnets can either attract each other strongly or repel each other strongly. Two magnets will go together as if made for each other if we are careful to put the north pole of one magnet with the south pole of the other magnet. When one of the magnets is turned around, however, north repels north and frustrates our efforts to push two like poles together.

The children of Adam are in a similar but much more profound dilemma. God has made us to worship him and has called us to worship him, the holy One. Yet, because of our sinfulness, we are automatically repelled by God's holiness, his alien beauty.

Many people do not understand the unseen force that causes God and man to repel, but the holiness of God and the sinfulness of his children repel each other as certainly as do the wrongly matched poles of two magnets. God created us for himself, to worship him and enjoy communion with him forever. Creator and creation, made in his likeness, should be drawn to each other. The cosmic tragedy is that we have become polarized from God by sin, especially by idolatry, which realigns our affections away from the God we were created to worship. Our worship of other gods of status, wealth, or fame reorients us away from God like a compass needle in an electrical storm is moved away from its orientation to true north. God's holiness repels us as surely as our sin repels him. As my son must learn how to couple the train, so we must learn how we can be reconnected to the Creator.

We have already seen from Scripture that members of Adam's fallen race rightly shrink from the presence of the true and living God. Isaiah was correct when he cried out: "Woe to me! . . . I am a man of unclean lips, and I live among a people of unclean lips, and my eyes have seen the King, the LORD Almighty" (6:5). In Ephesians Paul calls us God's natural "objects of wrath" (2:3). In Colossians we are described as his spiritual enemies (1:21). John Newton has not exaggerated. We are wretched, blind and lost.

This chapter will begin to explore the grand miracle of how God qualifies and transforms his spiritual enemies and the objects of his wrath to be his worshipers. Paul sums up the process succinctly: "He has qualified us." That miraculous change—from enemies to worshipers—is the essence of grace and the heart of our worship. The process by which he qualified us, and the experience of being qualified, also serve to energize and focus worship as we are brought into orbit around the throne of God.

Our proper worship of God hinges on a proper (if not deep) understanding of how this change is accomplished. The failure to understand "he qualified us" renders us unable to worship, and the implications of that failure extend throughout the church. Hebrews is emphatic: "Therefore, since we are receiving a kingdom that cannot be shaken, let us be thankful, and so worship God acceptably with reverence and awe, for our 'God is a consuming fire'" (12:28).

The dilemma of who can approach God as a worshiper is addressed by the psalmist:

> Who may ascend the hill of the LORD?
> Who may stand in his holy place?
> He who has clean hands and a pure heart,
>   who does not lift up his soul to an idol
>   or swear by what is false. [Ps. 24:3–4]

The question is straightforward: Who can possibly approach the holy God who created the world? The answer is twofold. First, to approach God, we must have pure hearts. Second, we must not worship a false god. We must worship the right God and we must approach him in the right way.

Worship—and any communion with God—requires a realignment of God's children to God, because in our fallen state we repel and are repelled by God's holiness. This process by which we are realigned in God's direction is the process of conversion. Art Gay, executive director of the World Relief Corporation, accurately describes conversion as "a total reorientation of the psyche towards God." It is as simple and yet as radical as realigning repelled and repelling magnets 180 degrees.

This process is God's doing and is the essence of God's work in human history. In 1 Thessalonians 1:9 (to which we shall return) Paul speaks of this reorientation: "They tell how you turned to God from idols to serve the living and true God." The Thessalonians were turned 180 degrees. They were first oriented toward the worship of false gods, which were part of the created world. Then they were reoriented toward God by the power of the Holy Spirit. Paul described the process: "For we know, brothers loved by God, that he has chosen you because our gospel came to you not simply with words, but also with power, with the Holy Spirit and with deep conviction" (1:4–5). That we should worship God at all is possible only because God has by the power of his Holy Spirit turned us fully around and enabled us to draw near to him.

Let's return for a moment to my son, frustrated with the wooden train that defies his attempt to connect the cars. There comes that moment when the freight car will be rightly attached to the engine and tears avoided only if I intervene on his behalf and turn the freight car around fully. The engine has a coupling magnet only at the rear. The freight cars have coupling magnets at each end, one north and one south. The freight car must be realigned to the engine or it will continue to repel the engine that is designed to pull it! The toy engine is the key—every car must be coupled in right relationship to the engine.

That God should by his Spirit realign us to be coupled with him spiritually in worship and in relationship is the miraculous central message of the gospel. It is the central message of grace. God is not realigned to us. We must be realigned to him. It is fully his work, described by Paul in the first half of Ephesians in wave after wave of blessing under the banner of "every spiritual blessing in Christ" (1:3):

"he chose us . . . to be holy and blameless" (1:4)
"he predestined us to be adopted as his sons" (1:4)
"in him we have redemption" (1:7)
"to bring all things . . . together under one head" (1:10)
"you also were included in Christ" (1:13)
"God raised us up with Christ and seated us with him" (2:6)
"you who once were far away have been brought near" (2:13)
"he has made the two one and has destroyed the barrier, the dividing wall of hostility" (2:14)
"you are no longer foreigners and aliens, but fellow citizens" (2:19)

All of this reminds us that it is God who, as an act of his grace, has enabled us to be his worshipers. He has lifted us and turned us around and reoriented us to himself. If we use the metaphor of the toy train, we see five important truths foundational to worship:

We were made to worship God.
Because sin and holiness repel each other, our relationship with God is broken and we are disconnected.
To be reconnected to God, God must turn us around 180 degrees and reorient us to himself.
The realignment toward God is totally of grace.
Therefore, grace is the foundation of our worship.

Worship always begins with the realignment of God's creation toward himself and celebrates that process of realignment.

Worship celebrates what C. S. Lewis rightly calls the "central event in all of human history": that God was in Christ reconnecting the world to himself. In what may seem like circular reasoning, worship is our celebration of being enabled to worship, it is our celebration of being restored to the place God created us to enjoy with him.

## Bestowing Grace on Ourselves

It has been more than fifty years since Dietrich Bonhoeffer warned that "cheap grace is the deadly enemy of our Church" because it erodes costly grace. Bonhoeffer's opening words are arresting:

> Cheap grace means grace sold on the market like cheapjacks wares. The sacraments, the forgiveness of sin, and the consolation of religion are thrown away at cut rate prices. . . . Grace without price; grace without cost! The essence of grace, we suppose, is that the account has been paid in advance; and, because it has been paid, everything can be had for nothing. Cheap grace means grace as a doctrine, a principle, as system. It means forgiveness of sins proclaimed as a general truth, the love of God taught as the Christian "conception" of God. An intellectual assent to that idea is held to be of itself sufficient to secure remission of sins.[1]

Bonhoeffer goes on to suggest that "cheap grace is the grace we bestow upon ourselves." It is not true grace but a fraud, a rhinestone mixed in with the crown jewels of the kingdom of God. The contrast Bonhoeffer makes is compelling. Cheap grace is "forgiveness without repentance, baptism without church discipline, communion without confession. Cheap grace is grace without discipleship, grace without the cross, grace without Jesus Christ. . . ."[2]

Bonhoeffer also gives us a sound theological anchor for our understanding of grace: "It is costly because it condemns sin, and grace because it justifies the sinner. . . . Above all it is grace because God did not reckon his son too dear a price to pay for our life, but delivered him up for us."[3]

Grace embodies all that God has done to reconcile sinful humanity and restore us to the position God intended for us as priests unto God. Without true grace that deals honestly with our infinite debt of sin and God's infinite provision in Christ, we do not have Christianity. Therefore, we do not have worship of the right God in the right way.

Grace makes worship possible and motivates worship. We have not favored God by scheduling a weekly time to worship him, but he has favored us by allowing us to come before him to worship. He has made it possible for us to be restored to the role of worshiper for which he created us: to glorify him. Only when we understand the enormity of that grace—grace that brought close those who were far off and brought to life those who were dead in sin—do we comprehend worship first as a privilege and then as a moral and just obligation. If we feel we have to worship God only as a duty, it is unlikely that we can worship at all because we have yet to apprehend grace.

Whether it is cheap grace or shallow grace, an inadequate understanding of grace is also the enemy of the church's calling to worship because inadequate teaching about grace does not squarely face the issue of sin. Shallow grace obviates the need to understand or confront the holiness of God.

## Don't Skimp on the Foundation

As a high-school student in Chicago I often drove into the city as part of my job. At that time the Hancock Building was under construction. For months I recall driving past the site and seeing lots of activity, but no progress. "Where is the building?" I wondered. I soon learned that in Chicago, where there is no bedrock to build on, a foundation of cassons must be poured deep into the ground. In the case of the eleven-hundred-foot Hancock Building, the cassons went down as far as the building went up. The same cannot be said for another famous building, a tower in Pisa. When the foundation is flawed, the superstructure will always list.

So it is with worship. Worship that is not established upon an understanding that a holy God has qualified his sinful created beings to worship him by his grace alone falls short of being worship of the right God in the right way. Worship of God built on any other foundation soon begins to reveal a distinct tilt. Much of what we call worship today reveals such a tilt.

The foundational problem of our present age is that our theology will fail to generate true worship of God if there is no understanding of who God is and who we are in relationship to his holiness. Without an understanding of holiness of the God who is a "consuming fire" there is no proper understanding of human sin. Without an understanding of sin there is no understanding of the totality of our consequential alienation from God. Without an understanding of the consequences of sin there is no understanding of grace. Without an understanding of grace, there is no proper motivation for worship—and nothing to celebrate. Without a proper motivation for worship we are left with either dead legalism and ritual or a human-centered substitute for true worship that never takes our focus off of ourselves and elevates it to God.

## An Erosion of the Foundation

As an incoming freshman in college I was part of a class that went through a major housing crisis. The new high-rise dormitory on campus, scheduled to open that fall of 1967, didn't. Just before the certificate of occupancy was to be signed, someone discovered that the fourteen-story building was not plumb. According to the unofficial version of the story, the engineers discovered that the building had been plumbed to the elevator shafts, but that the elevator shafts were not plumbed accurately. The story may be apocryphal, but the problem and the solution were not. When the foundation is not right, what can you do? The common answer is to accept the reality and live with it as long as and as well as possible. Under severe pressure to house the students, the college administrators made a pragmatic decision to allow students to move into the lower floors. Over the next few years all the remaining floors were gradually occupied. By the time the facility was fully occupied all of the class of 1971 had moved on. The history of the building and the question of its safety had faded away.

In a simiilar way, new wings of the church today are being built on a different foundation than the one established by God (1 Cor. 3:11). Churches are built on foundations of positive self-esteem and God's love proclaimed as a generalized truth, rather than on a message of sinful humanity and the grace of God. As floor upon floor is added to this structure, the questions about the foundation seem to be ignored, treated as irrelevant issues of history.

It is doubtful that anyone enjoys preaching about sin or sinfulness and the wretched spiritual condition of fallen people, but ultimately there is no reconciliation to God and no right worship of the right God without it.

Yet, we are living at a time when being politically correct is highly valued, and talking about sin is not politically correct.[4] The reality of that was underscored recently in the *Los Angeles Times*. A Presbyterian minister, the Reverend Roland Hughes, "rankled the Presbyterian Church" (PCUSA) by suggesting at the funeral for a homosexual AIDS victim that homosexuals (and heterosexuals) need to repent of their sexual sin. In response to a storm of protest, the Presbytery of Southern California relieved Hughes of his duties.[5]

Current literature about how to reach and minister to baby boomers unanimously suggests that the church find alternate terms for sin: for example, the great hymn "Amazing Grace" needs to be updated by dropping the line "saved a wretch like me." Today's generation, we are told, is interested in worshiping God, but is repelled by the church's traditional teachings on sin. Indeed, a secular publication, Newsweek, suggested recently that many "churches have discovered that 'low self-esteem' is a less off-putting phrase to congregants than 'sin.'"[6]—as though they are the same thing. Consequently, various circumlocutions are promoted: having low self-esteem, not living up to your potential, falling short, messing up, making bad choices, or making mistakes.

It seems hard to imagine that God destroyed Sodom and Gomorrah for not living up to the their potential. Or that Isaiah should cry out, "Woe to me! I have made poor choices and I live among a people of poor self-esteem!" Or that Jesus would have said the Holy Spirit "will convict the world of making mistakes, of righteousness and of judgment." We have come a long way from the people of God who wrote on their headgear *holy unto YHWH*.

Paul predicted this era of political correctness to Timothy: "For the time will come when men will not put up with sound doctrine. Instead, to suit their own desires, they will gather around them a great number of teachers to say what their itching ears want to hear" (2 Tim. 4:3). It is the faithful proclamation of God's Word and God's words—sin, righteousness, and judgment—that by the ministry of the Holy Spirit brings unbelievers to an awareness of their sin and to their knees in worship.

We must wonder what version of the Bible some contemporary evangelicals read when they contend that sin is not worth talking about in face of the risks of turning off this generation. In the second chapter of Ephesians, Paul, who elaborates in great detail the blessing bestowed on us in Christ, elaborates as fully the curse of sin upon us:

"you were dead in your transgressions and sins, in which
you used to live" (2:1)
"[we] were by nature objects of his wrath" (2:3)
"[we] were dead in transgressions" (2:5)
"you who were once far away" (2:13)

If God merely saved us from not living up to our potential, then salvation required only his love for his very lovable
people—but not his grace. Along this line of thinking, the
unmerited favor of God's grace is not needed because his
creation is *worthy* of his love. His creation is misguided perhaps, imperfect of course, but deserving of his love. So, when
God lifted us out of a slimy pit and set our feet on a solid
rock—as David exulted—it wasn't a very big step. This line
of thinking attracts many people because it preserves what
they consider to be their godly self-esteem, so important to
their overall well-being. This flawed reasoning proceeds to
the conclusion that the important esteem-giving truth of
God's love is compromised by harmful and unnecessary talk
about sin, being lost, being blind, and being a wretch.

The spiritual reality is something else, however. Only
when we understand how deep is the pit of our sin do we
understand how far the arm of the Lord reached down to
save us. Make no mistake, the love of God for his fallen creation, love that moved God to offer his own Son by his grace,
is far more to God's glory than is the love of God for basically good people who have merely made a few mistakes.

That is why we must guard the integrity of the drama of
redemption—complete with a full disclosure of our sinfulness and God's holiness—as the only proper foundation for
worship. Tampering with that drama to mimimize sin results
in minimizing God's grace, mimimizing his glory, and minimizing our worship.

# THE ENEMIES OF GRACE

It is no surprise that when today's
affluent young professionals return to
church, they want to do it only on their
own terms—what's amazing is how far
the churches are going to oblige.
—Katheleen Neumeyer,
"God For Sale,"
*Los Angeles Magazine*

## Eating Away as We Keep Writing

When I was a homeowner in the Southwest, I lived with
a constant awareness that my home could be under attack.
The unseen termite is native to sandy soils and climates where
there are no hard freezes to wipe him out. Built on a slab
poured rudely over the termite's ancestoral territory, my home
was vulnerable to attack. My best defense against the termite
required the constant and costly vigilance of a monthly pest
service that sought to maintain a protective barrier around
the perimeter of my home. But because I had a slab home,
there was no protection against infestation from under the
house.

For those who fail to protect against the infestation, the remedies can be severe. Most common is "tenting"—fumigating the entire house under the cover of a huge tent. Others have tried injecting liquid nitrogen into the wall cavities to freeze the termites, just as a visit to Frostbite Falls, Minnesota, might do. Left alone, the termite can destroy a frame home from within. It's only a matter of time.

The church is infested with spiritual termites. In the name of reaching the lost, we have invited into the church an infestation of politically correct theological bugs that have eaten away at the holiness of God, chewed holes in our understanding of grace, and weakened the structure of our worship and our Lord's church.

## Assessing the Damage

Ben Patterson anguishes over the damage done by these pests and the need to rebuild:

> The great awakenings in the country were hatched in worship. God's people began to be awe-struck by his majesty and holy love. It was not then as it is now, for we today seem interested only in his love, sans holiness and majesty. But the awakenings of the past linked love to a holy God. With this came holy fear, deep repentance, and confession of sin. Then with the cleansing work of the Holy Spirit came an outpouring of praise and intercession for sinners, which led to massive revival.[1]

Patterson is not alone. Francis Schaeffer wrote, "Here is the great evangelical disaster—the failure of the evangelical world to stand for truth as truth. . . . The evangelical world has accommodated the world spirit of the age."[2] Erwin Lutzer at Moody Church observes that "within evangelicalism there is a distressing drift toward accepting a Christianity that does not demand . . . [but makes] a growing accommodation—selecting what we like from the Bible and leaving the rest."[3] Because some have determined that the biblical teaching about the character of a holy God and the condition of fallen man is offensive, they have subordinated those doctrines to the more comfortable and comforting doctrine of the love of God.

It is little wonder that some of the prophetic voices of the church in the second half of this century are people who understand and are zealous for the holiness of God. Chuck Colson writes in *Loving God* that the messages of R. C. Sproul on the holiness of God—tapes he expected to be dry, dull theology —changed him: "By the end . . . I was on my knees, deep in prayer in awe of God's absolute holiness. It was a life-changing experience as I gained a new understanding of the holy God I believe and worship."[4]

The attack on the doctrines of the church that serve as the foundation for our worship—the holiness of God, the sinfulness of man, the grace of God—has not gone unnoticed. Even secular observers of the church have sounded a sympathetic alarm.

It was notable in 1975 when secular psychologist Karl Menninger asked the secular world why everyone had abandoned the concept of sin. Scott Peck challenged the psychiatric community with the reality of evil in *People of the Lie.*

A recent article in *Los Angeles Magazine* observed: "It is no surprise that when today's affluent young professionals return to church, they want to do it only on their own terms—what's amazing is *how far the churches are going to oblige*" (italics added).[5] The return of baby boomers to the church is measurable, but to attract them, or at least not to repel them, churches have to "air-brush sin." *Newsweek* religion editor Kenneth Woodward has observed the start of the same trend in the church. In "Pick and Choose Christian-

ity," a review of a Presbyterian-funded survey of Christians
in Minnesota, Woodward observed:

> [They] have developed a "pick and choose" Christianity in
> which individuals take what they want . . . and pass over what
> does not fit their spiritual goals.
>
> What many have left behind is a pervasive sense of sin.
> Although 98 percent said they believed in personal sin, only
> 57 percent accepted the traditional notion that all people
> are sinful and fully one-third allow that they "make many
> mistakes" but are not sinful themselves. Said one typical
> respondent: "The day I die, I should only have to look up at
> my Maker and say, 'Take me,' not 'forgive me.'"[6]

What sounds the loudest alarm is that the trend of watering
down the foundational biblical concept of sin is being
observed and reported by secular journalists. It is secular
journalists who have accused the church of "air-brushing"
sin. If Woodward did not fully grasp the implications of his
own concluding statement, evangelicals should: "Church is
now less a place where Christians worship God than an arena
where they wrestle with him."[7] The erosion of the church's
teaching of the doctrine of the sinfulness of fallen humanity
corresponds with a diminution of the doctrine of the holiness
of God.

A proper theology of worship is established on the foundations of God's grace and God's holiness. His grace makes
it possible for us sinful people to worship a holy God, and
an awareness of his holiness prompts our worship as we
understand the infinite nature of his love and grace.

## Selling Out to the Age

Perhaps the ministry of Terry Cole-Whittaker is an example of how far some people will accommodate the spirit of

the age at the price of biblical truth. Cole-Whittaker, a San Diego-based evangelist in the early 1980s, drew front-page attention in the *Wall Street Journal*. The *Journal* said of her: "The Rev. Terry is the evangelist to the yuppies . . . she preaches a gospel of 'happiness now' to her congregation of young urban professionals." Her church of two thousand people had a television ministry in a number of United States markets and a glowing testimony of her impact from the National Religious Broadcasters. Yet, her theology reflected an odyssey away from a United Methodist upbringing through the positive thinking of Religious Science Church and then to an independent ministry. "Sin is self-hatred," "hell is what some of us build for ourselves right here on earth," and the teaching of an afterlife for "all eternal cosmic beings" are the foundations of her theology. It was no secret among the ministry staff that pragmatism, not theological truth, was the foundation for her ministry: "Terry's secret is simple: She always tells everyone they're wonderful and exactly what they want to hear."[8]

The value of Cole-Whittaker, who was on the religious scene for only a brief moment, is that she defined for us self-centered religion. Her message was transparently contrary to the Word of God. Although she referred to herself as a "metaphysical, evangelical, pentecostal space cadet," San Diego pastors knew exactly what she was: "quasi-religious at best," and the purveyor of a self-centered religion of positive thinking. It is a faith without teaching about sin because there is no holy One to give definition to sin by his own holy character. There is no God worthy of worship, and no grace—or need for grace—to energize that worship.

The importance of this self-described "pentecostal space cadet" is the understanding that she gives about the direction theology will float when it is cut loose from its biblical mooring. Apart from the revelation of God, fallen humanity creates religions and gods in its own image.[9] Cole-

Whittaker admits severing her ties to orthodoxy because she hated having "Jesus and the Bible forced down [her] throat." It is, therefore, simple to tell that this particular Californian is not in the evangelical camp. Unfortunately, it is not as easy to notice the theological drift of others who claim the name *evangelical* but who have also cut themselves adrift from their orthodox biblical moorings.

In Southern California, seismologists are interested in measuring the slightest drift of geological plates. The movement of these tectonic plates along fault lines causes earthquakes and will some day cause the "big one" as the coastal plate slides north along the continental shelf from Los Angeles to San Francisco. Consequently, seismologists at Cal Tech and the U.S. Geologic Survey have installed sensitive laser instruments along the San Andreas (and other) fault lines to measure even the slightest movement.[10] Detecting the slightest movement is costly and difficult, but it is essential because the welfare of millions of people is at stake.

Being able to detect slight theological drift is important, too. The eternal welfare of millions of people is at stake. Almost any knowledgable evangelical can see how far Cole-Whittaker has drifted from the orthodox doctrines of evangelical Christianity. It is much more important to be able to detect doctrinal drift when it is not so obvious.

Almost any person, for example, who rose at sunrise, had breakfast, later gets hungry, and observes that the sun is overhead, knows at once that his or her watch is wrong if it still reads 7:42 A.M. This individual should rightly expect it to read 11:42 A.M. The earlier reading is so far off that it is obviously wrong. Yet, if the watch is off by only thirty minutes—11:42 A.M. when it is actually 12:12 P.M.—there is a more serious problem: the watch is wrong, but it is not obviously wrong. The thirty minutes could mean missing an appointment, missing a wedding, or, on some airlines, missing a flight departure!

Not everyone who chews away at the orthodox teachings of our faith is as obvious as Cole-Whittaker. In this past year a rising star in Southern California evangelical circles spoke to an audience of Christian families at a weekend camp. So committed and so well-versed in political correctness was this "dynamic young communicator" that he never used the word *sin*, even to a Christian audience in a message he said was about the character of the holy God. He didn't use any of the offensive vocabulary, but drew totally from the modern lexicon of alternative words and phrases.

We want to avoid purposely blowing away non-Christians with "Sinner, are you saved?" But, have we not seriously damaged the doctrine of the holiness of God by speaking of his holiness as the "wow!" of God? Have we not eaten into the right understanding of our human condition by calling sin the "ouch" caused by "not living up to our potential"? The damage done in the name of being relevant is as real as the damage done by the false prophet who willfully deceives.

When we let down our guard, the termites will eat at our doctrinal framework until the whole roof caves in. We must agree with Neumeyer that it is amazing how far the church is willing to go to accommodate a generation that is interested in God on its own terms. We will see in the next chapter that this is not new. Men and women have been tampering with the truth about God almost from the beginning, seeking to find a way to approach the holy God on their terms rather than on his. The appeal of finding God on our terms, with our pride intact and not needing his unmerited favor, is not new.

# ALTERNATIVES TO GRACE

In an age determined to judge everything by quantifications and statistics, it
should come as no surprise that mar-
keters and demographers pretend to
plumb the mysteries of God's grace.
—Rodney Clapp
"Give Me that Old-time Pragmatism,"
*Wall Street Journal*

## Vision or Revision of God

For my generation, the baby boomers, a reprint of Jonathan Edwards's "Sinners in the Hands of an Angry God" was standard fare in a high-school American literature class. It seems as if this one message from the Puritans was selected for anthologies because, without proper contextualization, it had the greatest potential for offending the modern American mind and undermining the historic orthodox view of the holy and righteous God. I recall Edwards being discussed in class not with scorn or contempt, but with smug amusement that people "back then" could have believed such a view of God. That concept of God, the teacher sug-

103

gested, was just a product of the biblical literalism of the times—a sort of theological buggy whip that no longer serves a purpose.

We need a modern God, a figurehead God acceptable to sophisticated and erudite Americans. We need a God we can passively acknowledge on our currency and coinage but who does not threaten our way of life. So the God of the Puritans needed to be re-engineered to get rid of unacceptable defects like his holiness, his anger, and especially, his eternal judgment.

I have watched with interest as scholars, both real and self-proclaimed, have grappled with the task of domesticating God. They are forever seeking to find alternatives to grace, so they can approach him on favorable terms of merit rather than on terms of unconditional favor.

When a magnet loses its magnetic force, it ceases to repel other magnets. But it also ceases to strongly attract. Perhaps when the perception of God's holiness is diminished and no longer repels, God no longer attracts us with the same intensity either. Grace without an understanding of sin and God's holiness is not grace at all. Grace without sin does not draw us toward God. Many scholars, however, seem to prefer weakened theological magnets that neither repel nor attract. Weakened doctrines offer alternatives to grace and suggest that not-so-sinful people can be restored in their relationships with not-so-holy God by some way other than God's unmerited favor and intervention.

Other scholars have drafted new theologies that acknowledge the absolute holiness of God in principle, but suggest that grace is not enough to gain standing before God. They offer supplements to grace as the means by which we may stand before God. Mystical spiritism, religion, and philosophy substitute for grace. These are not new approaches into the presence of God, but false answers as old as the oldest book in the Bible.

Because our current confusion over worship is rooted at least in part in the watering down of the holiness of God and the down-playing of sin in the name of reaching the unfound (we should avoid the word *lost*), it may be worthwhile to seek out the headwaters of this current of revisionism.

## The Sources of Modern Revisionism

An examination of Job, the oldest book in the Bible, serves us well here. Amidst all of Job's suffering we find a remarkable debate between Job and his three friends, Zophar, Bildad, and Eliphaz. The issue is often thought to be that of suffering, or more specifically, why good people suffer. But closer examination reveals that the central question is quite different. That central question for debate is found in Job 9:2:

"Indeed, I know that this is true.
*But how can a mortal be righteous before God?*
Though one wished to dispute with him,
he could not answer him one time out of a thousand.
His wisdom is profound, his power is vast.
Who has resisted him and come out unscathed?
He moves mountains without their knowing it
and overturns them in his anger." [Job 9:2–5, italics added]

Then Job correctly concludes in 9:32: "He is not a man like me that I might answer him, that we might confront each other in court."

Job and his friends were theologically correct in their general understanding of the holiness of God. Holiness implies not only moral perfection but also the otherness of God. He is distinct from his creation. He is not human. We do not speak God's name by shouting "Man!" This ancient council convened in sackcloth and ashes understood that no one on his own is righteous before God.

Not even Job with his apparent righteousness (God had said to Satan there was no one like Job, upright and righteous before God) has standing before the holy and sovereign Creator. Job and his friends seek to understand not only Job's suffering but also his standing before God. After all, if a person who appears righteous must still shrink away from the holiness of God, who can possibly stand in his presence?

Job's friends respond to Job's suffering and to his question with three fallacious arguments about how a person can be righteous before God. They argue that anyone can ascend the hill of the Lord if he has the right equipment, understands the right teaching, or has the right preparation. They speculate that humans can approach God as worshipers by offering solutions of their own to the problem of righteousness.

From Bildad comes the alternative to grace called philosophy:

"Ask the former generations
    and find out what their fathers learned,
for we were born only yesterday and know nothing,
    and our days on earth are but a shadow.
Will they not instruct you and tell you?
    Will they not bring forth words from their understanding?
Can papyrus grow tall where there is no marsh?
    Can reeds thrive without water?
While still growing and uncut,
    they wither more quickly than grass.
Such is the destiny of all who forget God;
    so perishes the hope of the godless." [8:8–13]

Bildad appeals to the great thinkers of the day. Arguing that our understanding of the world should be shaped by those who have come before, he asserts that correct contemporary philosophy must always grow out of the ideas of the past.

Bildad warns against forgetting God but leaves the former generations to answer the question of how a mortal can stand before God.

It would appear that evangelicalism today has allowed its thinking to be influenced, if not shaped, by the major philosophical movements of the late nineteenth and the twentieth centuries as well as by the philosophical processes that guided those movements. The current age of neopaganism has been shaped by several ideologies passed down by our fathers in the last century.

Charles Darwin has impacted the church not so much with his theory of evolution as stated in *The Origin of Species* (1848), but with the applications of his theories into social categories. For a century and a half before Darwin, rationalism had been dispensing salvos against three philosophical tenets of Christianity: revelation, miracles, and God's Word as the only sound basis for human conduct. Darwin, stunned by the impact of his own work, was to bring to an end in the West a world view that allows for the supernatural. Although I do not fully agree with all of the conclusions of secular history, the role assigned to Darwin cannot be seriously challenged:

> Over a perspective of a longer span of time, however, much of the trial and torment aroused by the challenge of Darwinism to religion appears to be one version of a recurring and never resolved struggle. In the seventeenth century—to go back no further—a struggle between traditional faith and the avant-garde criticism of miracles had been vigorously waged. This battle was repeated in new variations, during the height of the 18th century enlightenment, and again in the Darwinian era. Each time, one may believe, there was a loss of faith. But each time, the lines reformed, with differing religious responses. In our own time a modernist Christianity, fully at home with Darwinism, has survived; and it coexists with what we have come to call fundamentalist Christianity, which is still based upon Biblical literalism.[1]

It is impossible to measure the overall impact of Darwin on our culture and the degree to which he has influenced the evangelical church. The most pervasive influence seems to be the acceptance of the scientific method as the basis of truth and the source of knowledge. Never mind that logical positivism—that truth is the product of careful and repeated observation of phenomena—is a phenomenon that itself cannot be proven by careful and repeated scientific observation. Darwin has shaped the a priori of our culture, which has in turn influenced even the evangelical church.

Sigmund Freud's influence is also more pervasive than his contribution, dubious though it may be, of psycho-analysis. Freud's ideas and vocabulary have become part of Western culture. The greatest impact may have come from Freud's redefinition of guilt. Christians will admit that many people experience false guilt; Freud moved Western thought toward the pronouncement that all guilt is false guilt. The evangelical church continues to have a dreadful time of deal-ing with real and false guilt in accordance with biblical prin-ciples,[2] a struggle that is a consequence of the pervasive influence of Freud and of our inability to mount a consis-tent counteroffensive.

In the first part of this century the theories of John Dewey became widely accepted. This founder of progressive edu-cation may have done more than anyone to advance the idea that humankind is basically good. Built on both Freud and Darwin, this humanist doctrine of mankind's basic goodness has permeated the culture and has left its mark on the evan-gelical church. A person is not sinful, in need of a savior; a person is misguided and in need of a teacher. Secular con-trol of the public educational system of the United States has steadily increased since the 1830s, and continues today, more or less without opposition. Dewey's ideology has greatly influenced a whole culture, even though few people know precisely what his ideology was.

Although not many American evangelicals care to be conversant about existentialism, this philosophical construct of the twentieth century shapes both our culture and the church in profound ways. The names of Sarte and Camus spark memories of literature classes, but the broad influence of existentialism belies the narrow literary impact of their fiction. Born out of the despair of a Europe that had experienced two world wars and a decade of depression, existentialism tore down classic liberalism, the last in a series of philosophic systems to reign over Western culture. For the existentialist, every foundation for meaningful civilization has been discredited: the church, reason, rationalism, the monarchy, liberalism. The world is not evolving. The dialectical materialism of Marx and Hegel (thesis—antithesis—synthesis) is not bringing a better world.

The despair of existentialism brought a new philosophy that has flourished well in the soil of American individualism, the philosophy that every person is the ultimate judge of truth, for nothing can be true unless and until it is individually experienced and individually validated. More than twenty-five years ago, David Hubbard of Fuller Seminary pointed to the implications of existentialism. While many scholars in the turbulent late 1960s and early 1970s pointed to an erosion of authority, Hubbard argued instead that the culture was witnessing an internalization of authority consistent with existential thought. The internalization of authority ("I am an authority unto myself") is the logical manifestation of existentialism.[3]

Were we, then, to take Bildad's measured counsel and look to our fathers (not Bildad's fathers), they would conclude that Job is basically good and not in need of reconciliation to God. God may have created the world and its natural laws (the view of the Enlightenment philosophers) but is not involved in the day-to-day operation of the cosmos. Job's sufferings are part of the process of natural selection in which the fit will survive and the weak will perish. His suffering is unrelated to a God who has placed the whole of creation under a curse because of sin.

Listening to our ancestors to see what they have to say about our relationship to God is fraught with peril. Those ancestors have perpetuated numerous errors about how mortals can stand before a righteous God. Led astray by faulty responses to human suffering, Bildad's adherents fail to come to grips with the question for many reasons: they deny sin and its consequences, they deny revelation as authoritative, and they even suggest that God exists only if he exists for you.

From Eliphaz comes spiritism (or animism) as an alternative to grace:

"A word was secretly brought to me,
    my ears caught a whisper of it.
Amid disquieting dreams in the night,
    when deep sleep falls on men,
fear and trembling seized me
    and made all my bones shake.
A spirit glided past my face,
    and the hair on my body stood on end.
It stopped,
    but I could not tell what it was.
A form stood before my eyes,
    and I heard a hushed voice:
'Can a mortal be more righteous than God?
    Can a man be more pure than his Maker?'" [4:12–17]

Eliphaz's response opens a huge portal through which all manner of false teachings can enter under the pretense of religion. Although the phantom asks the right question, we cannot know the identity of the spirit. Eliphaz assumes that if it is a spirit, it must speak for God; but that is not so. The spirit's visit leads Eliphaz away from grace to spiritism as the basis for our standing before God. This view is akin to the teachings of the first-century gnostics, who promoted the heresy addressed by so many of the New Testament epistles. The gnostic taught that a person needed to be initiated into a secret spiritual truth in order to understand God. God revealed knowledge (*gnosis*) to those spiritually deserving persons who demonstrated their spirituality by denial or by renouncing all flesh, which is evil. The asceticism of the gnostic was rewarded by initiation into deeper and deeper spiritual secrets. There were, then, spiritual haves and spiritual have-nots, resulting in the development of an identifiable spiritual hierarchy. Our closeness to God and the blessings that accrue are the consequence of our accumulated spiritual experience, not a consequence of grace.

We do not need to go very far out on a limb to find mysticism, monism, and Eastern pantheism in this New Age. Shirley MacLaine and others have already told us that we are God and that the path to God is inward. We are to believe that because we are God, we do not need to be reconciled to him. Mystics do not need channels to God; they are channels to God.

Our evangelical subculture is rampant with a form of mysticism and superspiritualism, demonstrated by the televangelists who relish "slaying people in the Spirit" by breathing on them or by striking them with a garment. They project a superspirituality to an audience of—by implication—spiritual inferiors in order to maintain their ministry and cash flow. The distorted teaching that "we are little gods" is a bold-faced claim to spiritual superiority. Spiritual status in some circles is determined by the number of mystical experiences, words of knowledge, visions, prophecies, and victorious

encounters with demons we have had. While most evangelicals readily acknowledge that spiritual gifts are all valid
because a sovereign God can do as he wills, there is great
danger in the theological teaching and activities of some
superspiritual figures of the Pentecostal movement. Their
doctrine and their practice reveal them to have more in common with modern manifestations of gnosticism than with
historic Christianity.

We do not stand before the holy God by means of mystical spiritual experience. Moreover, there is neither a set of
concentric circles to navigate into spirituality, nor a ladder
of hierarchy to super-Christianity to climb with each new
mystical experience.

It is not hard to speculate that Eliphaz may well have
considered himself to be spiritually superior to the others
because the spirit visited him. Eliphaz revealed the future.
He has told us not how to be righteous before God, but how
to be puffed up before God—proud of one's spiritual experiences, prowess, power, or position.

Religion, another alternative to grace, is introduced by
Zophar, who suggested the false but appealing answer of
self-salvation:

> "Yet if you devote your heart to him
>     and stretch out your hands to him,
> if you put away the sin that is in your hand
>     and allow no evil to dwell in your tent,
> then you will lift up your face without shame;
>     you will stand firm and without fear." [11:13–15]

Zophar suggested that anyone can stand before a holy God
by the process and effort of personal reformation or self-
salvation.

Advancing such a suggestion begins with the false
assumption that a sinful person is able to seek God, to put

away his own sin, and to devote himself to God. Zophar failed to grasp the nature of the fall into sin. Sin is not just wrongs for which a person needs to be forgiven. Sin has penetrated and corrupted every aspect of Adam's race, bringing death to the will, the intellect, the emotions, and the body. No spiritually dead person, then, searches for God. The answer to our problem of sin cannot begin with merely devoting ourselves to him.

Zophar also suggested that one need only clean oneself up and put away sin. Here Job's friend again fails to understand sin as an enslaving power in our lives. Jesus said that everyone who commits sin is a slave to sin. It is naive to think that sinful persons can put off their sin and allow no more to come into their lives, but that is Zophar's solution to the problem of sin.

The answer of religion is the organized self-effort of sinful people to satisfy (or at least to appease) a holy God. It puts the huge responsibility for expiation on the shoulders of sinners but also leaves religious people thinking they are fully in control of their spiritual situation. The attraction of being in control and the appeal to basic human pride are the primary lures of religion and self-salvation. All religions, even the religion we have made out of Christianity, are based on human effort as the means for establishing or reestablishing our relationship to God.

Religion does not square with true Christianity because it fails to confront the biblical assessment of sin, the biblical view of the perfect holiness of God, and the miracle of infinite grace that alone can reconcile sinful humans to a holy God.

## The Triumph of Grace

Although Job asked how to be righteous before God, he alone had even a clue as to the right answer:

"If only there were someone to arbitrate between us,
    to lay his hand upon us both,
someone to remove God's rod from me,
    so that his terror would frighten me no more.
Then I would speak up without fear of him,
    but as it now stands with me, I cannot." [9:33–35]

Job recognized that if he were to stand before God, someone would have to arbitrate or negotiate between him and God. He longed for someone who could "lay his hand upon us both." We cannot know what Job understood as he said this, but what he longed for—a God/Man who could touch Job because he also was a man and could touch God because he himself was divine—would come in the person of Jesus Christ. Only Jesus can arbitrate between a sinner and God because he alone is both fully the eternal God and, through his incarnation, fully and forever man. Little wonder Paul would say: "There is one God and one mediator between God and man, the man Christ Jesus."

The three false answers of Bildad, Eliphaz, and Zophar to the question of how to be righteous before God only serve to show how radical is the message of grace. Sinful humans and holy God are so totally separated and the effects of sin are so pervasive that no solution that involves the will, the intellect, the initiative, or the perception of humans will ever stand. Only the solution that is born in the will of God will solve the riddle of how to be righteous before God.

Watering down the holiness of God is a common element in all the various attempts to change the basis of our relationship with God. If only the holy One of Israel could be modified or re-engineered to accommodate the contemporary mind, people argue, then God could be approached and worshiped on any number of human terms. Then many more people could seek and find God—never mind that it is not on his terms! After all, isn't bringing people to God the goal?

As the American church seeks to establish consensus about worship and how to encompass unbelievers, it must not lose its bearings in the fog of contemporary thought. Without the fixed navigational points of God's absolute holiness, our total sinfulness, and God's infinite grace, it is impossible for us to find our way theologically. This erosion of the teaching of the holiness of God has made possible the spread of a "gospel," but it is a gospel stripped of grace. In the following chapter we will confront another threat to a gospel of grace that undermines worship, the various expressions of "grace plus."

# A PRESCRIPTION FOR GRACE 7

Dumbing down is like a disease. It
spreads and takes over and makes us less
and less capable as thinking people.
Dumbing down makes us easy victims of
shortsightedness, targets for manipu-
lation and control. Dumbing down is
the opposite of what the Apostle Paul
said when he pleaded with believers in
Jesus Christ: "do not conform any longer
to the pattern of this world, but be transformed by the renewing of your mind." It
can happen in church when we want to
"feel good" rather than come to grips with
God and the depths of the scriptures that
can anchor us when emotions fail—as
they always will in spite of ever more
dramatic experiences.
—Roger Palms,
"Dumbing,"
*Decision*

## Grace and Worship

Every pastor continually deals with a whole range of issues
caused by the breakdown of grace in the church. A critical

spirit, a spirit hatched in shallow grace, is sweeping through hundreds of churches today and destroying pastors and others in ministry. The lack of what Chuck Swindoll calls a "grace awakening"[1] has left many in the church gripped in a barren ice age of legalism. Modern Pharisees—the Abominable Snowmen who are forever at home in the environment of legalism—seem to be lurking everywhere. Negativism, divisiveness, and dysfunctional families and churches are common when true grace has not brought a thaw. The ice will not recede until the church experiences a grace awakening that enables members of the body of Christ to treat each other with real grace.

The church so often needs to experience and understand that true grace is a bold, life-changing reality that heals self-concept and binds up wounds left unhealed by conditional acceptance. In addition, the shallow experience of grace so common among modern evangelicals is at the heart of the church's spiritual infertility: ninety to ninety-five persons out of one hundred who profess the name of Christ have never led another person to Christ. My empirical studies of the psychological factors that affect the practice of witnessing point to the limited experience of grace as a primary reason that Christians so inadequately share their faith.[2] Most interesting and surprising was the evidence that when Christians are trained to share their faith in Christ (using the Navigators' well-known Bridge Illustration, one of several fine conventional methodologies), the impact may in a significant number of cases be negative. After they received evangelism training, many laypeople actually perceived themselves to be less competent, perceived the task to be more difficult, and perceived the non-Christian world more hostile than before. The only conclusion I could draw was that training people who were not properly motivated by a deep experience of grace to share their faith only increased their guilt for not doing so.

Witnessing has always been a duty for many church members, and an onerous one to some. Once they had been trained, many no longer had a a valid reason for not witnessing. Consequently they became loaded with additional guilt. The measurable shift in perceived difficulty of witnessing and the perceived resistance to the gospel reveal that trained witnesses used these reasons to rationalize why they were still not witnessing. Without the transforming power of God's grace, witnessing will remain an obligation subject to all the subtle inflictions of that guilt. Without grace, the church lacks the proper life-giving reason for its proclamation of the gospel.

While shallow grace today afflicts church members in many ways, the concern here is the damage done to our worship by a shallow understanding of grace. Without grace our emotions may be diseased, and without a grace reformation our witness may be impaired. But, without an avalanche of grace our worship will be damaged. It is important to consider that even as many are unaware of how the lack of grace has poisoned them emotionally or spiritually, the same unawareness extends to worship. Perhaps Swindoll sums up the cumulative effect of this dearth of grace:

> Too many folks are being turned off by a twisted concept of the Christian life. Instead of offering a winsome and contagious, sensible and achievable invitation of hope and cheer through the sheer power of Christ, more people than ever are projecting a grim-faced caricature of religion on demand [another term for Bonhoeffer's cheap grace]. I find it tragic that religious kill-joys have almost succeeded in taking the freedom and fun out of faith. People need to know that there is more to the Christian life than deep frowns, pointing fingers, and unrealistic expectations.[3]

The grace reformation—needed to transform our lives and revive our worship—is amply developed in the Olivet Discourse in John 15:1–11:

"I am the true vine, and my Father is the gardener. He cuts off every branch in me that bears no fruit, while every branch that does bear fruit he prunes so that it will be even more fruitful. You are already clean because of the word I have spoken to you. Remain in me, and I will remain in you. No branch can bear fruit by itself; it must remain in the vine. Neither can you bear fruit unless you remain in me.

"I am the vine; you are the branches. If a man remains in me and I in him, he will bear much fruit; apart from me you can do nothing. If anyone does not remain in me, he is like a branch that is thrown away and withers; such branches are picked up, thrown into the fire and burned. If you remain in me and my words remain in you, ask whatever you wish, and it will be given you. This is to my Father's glory, that you bear much fruit, showing yourselves to be my disciples.

"As the Father has loved me, so have I loved you. Now remain in my love. If you obey my commands, you will remain in my love, just as I have obeyed my Father's commands and remain in his love. I have told you this so that my joy may be in you and that your joy may be complete."

Although the word *grace* does not appear in this passage, the message of grace and its impact on our lives reverberates through it. To see the beauty of this passage, a many-faceted gem of our faith, it may be helpful to see the background against which this treasure is set. The principles given by Jesus in John are in vivid contrast to what Paul calls the "world's principles,"[4] principles antithetical to grace.

At the heart of our being is our genuine need to be known intimately and still be loved. In our modern society the universal need for love and unconditional acceptance is pursued at every turn, albeit pursued wrongly. The world's principles lie to us and tell us that achievement and possessions will provide status. If we can make more money, buy a bigger home, have imported luxury cars with car phones (a must!), vacation in the right places (unencumbered by children), we will have status in our culture. Our identity and our worth are welded by our culture to what we do vocationally, not to who we are ontologically. The axioms imply that if we possess or accomplish enough, we will gain status. So, if we possess or attain more, we will gain even more status and establish our identity. We think that we will be somebody by doing something or by having something.

Status, we are told, will bring acceptance and self-esteem. If we can "be somebody," the world instructs, we can position ourselves to grab the brass ring of acceptance. And, of course, the greater the status, the greater the acceptance.

Granted, there is a basic human struggle between being and doing, a struggle that is demonstrated by the story of Mary and Martha. Mary was concerned with being—being at the feet of Jesus. Martha was concerned with doing all the tasks incumbent upon a hostess. The two orientations came into conflict. In our culture also the focus seems to be on doing rather than on being. This is reflected in our custom of asking people we meet what they do!

### Illustration 7.1
*Living According to the World's Principles*

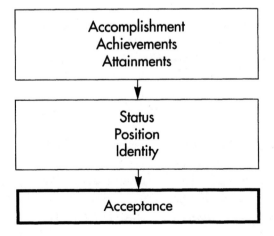

Accomplishment
Achievements
Attainments

Status
Position
Identity

Acceptance

122 The Role of Grace in the Christian Life

There are several problems with this beyond the basic realization that the Bible calls these principles sin because they claim to fulfill people apart from their Creator. First John 2:16 reminds us that these worldly principles are the opposite of kingdom values: "For everything in the world—the cravings of sinful man, the lust of his eyes and the boasting of what he has and does—comes not from the Father but from the world." The deepest longing of our hearts comes not at the end of the process, but at the beginning.

As Jeff VanVonderen observed in *Tired of Trying to Measure Up,* the world's principles have polluted the church and will continue to pollute the church until grace dissolves or absorbs the pollutants of this wrong thinking:

> Never before have so many spiritually tired Christians been wounded and in need of counseling.
>
> Trying hard is not the solution. When someone becomes a Christian he has a brand new identity as a child of God because of the cross of Christ. But the truth is, people are affirmed in our society, in families and even in our churches for what they do, not for who they are. When a person comes into a relationship with Christ, most of the teaching he receives is about how Christians are supposed to act, not who a Christian is as a new creation in Christ.[5]

So, while we may preach the concept of grace, there appears to be a significant gap between the doctrine of grace we profess and the experience of grace we live out. It is the gap between being and doing. It is the gap caused by the incursion of the world's principles into the church, where these principles take root and produce the fruit of legalism, guilt, and shame. And even when these fruits are not fully in season, the world's principles, like the roots of a tall oak, crack the foundation on which the church is built.

The most common fruit of the world's principles to grow in the church is "grace plus." What is it that makes us acceptable, valuable people? We're often taught that acceptability comes from "useful" religious performance that lives up to the expectations of our particular religious community. So while our overt verbal message from the pulpit may repeatedly be one of grace, the subculture of the church continually sends a contradictory, even double-binding, covert message that acceptance is fully achieved not by grace, but by grace plus—grace plus "being a good Christian" as defined by our particular church.

Once again the result is a shallow and inadequate understanding of grace that will forever fail to transform God's people. This understanding is almost the opposite of cheap grace: this shallow understanding of grace seems to suggest that our sin is so horrible or so extensive that the cross, God's floodgate of grace, is not sufficient and must be supplemented by religious performance. This subtle pollution of the church by the world's principle of "accomplishment—status—acceptance" has eroded the church's adequate foundation of grace since Paul first warned the Colossians against such principles. This erosion of grace cannot help but undermine worship because worship, then, originates not in grace but in religious duty. The cross is not seen as sufficient reason for celebration because its effectiveness is diminished by the amount of religious duty we must perform to be accepted.

Grace must be the starting point for not only our worship but also our health. Jesus first pointed his disciples to wholeness by telling them that he had already accepted them unconditionally because of the grace ministered by his word: "I am the true vine, and my Father is the gardener. . . . You are already clean because of the word I have spoken to you" (John 15:1, 3).

Jesus begins with grace! We are already clean because the Word of God has come to us as Paul describes in 1 Thessalonians 1:5, "our gospel came to you not simply with words, but also with power, with the Holy Spirit and with deep conviction." Sinful children have been made clean not by anything they have done, but by the Word of God. That is grace!

Second, Jesus reminds his disciples that this grace continues to be theirs as they nurture their relationship to him: "Remain in me, and I will remain in you. No branch can bear fruit by itself; it must remain in the vine. Neither can you bear fruit unless you remain in me" (15:4). Grace is to be continually experienced in the context of our ongoing relationship with our Savior. Too many Christians have lost the measure of grace in their lives by not maintaining a love relationship, often because the daily quiet time was taught as a duty rather than a privilege to be cherished. It is unfortunate that our initial experience of grace doesn't come date-stamped like our cartons of milk. If it did perhaps we would replace it with fresh grace regularly.

Third, Jesus told us that our status and identity derive not from our accomplishments, but from our relationship with him: "I am the vine; you are the branches. . . . Apart from me you can do nothing" (15:5). That is our identity, our status. He is the Vine. We, by his grace, are his branches. That should not be taken as demeaning. A study of the Old Testament will reveal that Israel was the vine of God symbolized by the massive gold-plated vine encircling the main door of the temple in Jerusalem. We are the branches!

Fourth, Jesus told us that out of our identity as his branches would come our accomplishments (for the kingdom): "If a man remains in me and I in him, he will bear much fruit. . . . This is to my Father's glory, that you bear much fruit, showing yourselves to be my disciples" (15:5, 8). The world's principles have been turned around a full 180 degrees. What we do flows out of who we are—the gracious position we possess in Christ: "We are his workmanship, created in Christ Jesus unto good works which God has ordained for us in advance." It is only at the end that the focus turns to doing and away from being. Our works are never in place of or a supplement to grace—they are a response to the continual understanding and experience of grace (see illustration 7.2).

This model[6] Jesus gives for spiritual, mental, and emotional health, a model that is based totally and exclusively upon grace. Our acceptance comes from God by grace. That relationship establishes our identity, who we are; and out of who we are flow all the things we do. The values of the kingdom of God are poles apart from the Western culture in which we are submerged. Consequently, God is far more concerned about faithfulness than about success—a seemingly simple matter that has become a sticking point for church members today. This dynamic process then leads into health and into joy: "I have told you this so that my joy may be in you and that your joy may be complete" (15:11).

## Real Grace, the Key to Right Worship

Grace is also the only proper foundation, then, for the right worship of the right God. Worship is a barometer of our spiritual health and vitality, the degree to which we have continued to assimilate through our relationship with Christ the grace that first of all "called us out of darkness into his marvelous light." God has through Christ, by grace, called out of the darkness of sin and into his light each of us in order that we might "declare the praises" of the one who answered in the cross the question of who is qualified to worship God. Paul summarizes what the grace of God has done for us:

> bearing fruit in every good work, growing in the knowledge of God, being strengthened with all power according to his glo-

## Illustration 7.2
### *Living According to God's Principles*

> **[2] Nurture of Our Relationship**
>
> "Remain in me and I will remain in you. . . . If you remain in me and my words remain in you, ask whatever you wish and it will be given you."

> **[1] Acceptance**
>
> "You are clean because of the word I have spoken to you."

> **[3] Identity and Status**
>
> "No branch can bear fruit by itself; it must remain in the vine . . . I am the vine and you are the branches."

> **[4] Accomplishment/ Attainment**
>
> "This is to my father's glory, that you bear much fruit, showing yourselves to be my disciples."

rious might so that you may have great endurance and patience, and joyfully giving thanks to the Father, who has qualified you to share in the inheritance of the saints in the kingdom of light. For he has rescued us from the dominion of darkness and brought us into the kingdom of the Son he loves, in whom we have redemption, the forgiveness of sins. [Col. 1:10–14]

This inheritance as children of God is the great and awesome privilege of worshiping God for all eternity. He has qualified us by grace through Christ to be his worshipers! John's revelation informs us that by grace we have been made "to be a kingdom and priests to serve our God." John is so overwhelmed at this reality that he is barely able to contain himself: "How great is the love the Father has lavished on us, that we should be called children of God! And that is what we are! . . . now we are children of God, and what we will be has not yet been made known. But we know that when he appears, we shall be like him, for we shall see him as he is" (1 John 3:1–2).

In chapter 2 we noted that God is both qualified to be worshiped and the qualifier of worshipers from the race of Adam. God is worthy of worship from every creature; should we not find in the entire program of God in history to qualify us to be his worshipers and his children a veritable springboard into worship?

Again and again the pages of the New Testament confirm the ontology—we are the children of God by his grace. In Romans 8 Paul repeats it several times to make sure we don't miss the concept of who we are in Christ:

those who live by the Spirit of God are sons of God
you received the spirit of sonship
"by him we cry '*Abba*, Father'" (8:15)
"the Spirit . . . testifies with our spirit that we are God's children" (8:16)
"heirs of God and co-heirs with Christ" (8:17)

The repetition might border on monotony if it were not so grand and so crucial. We are what we are by the grace of God: people qualified forever to be worshipers of the true and living God. Then we shall fulfill God's purpose for creating us: that we might glorify God and enjoy him forever. But God's grace has not only qualified us to worship, it is also our reason for worship. We are enabled to worship, and we have something worthy of praising God for all eternity.

Christians who have not fully grasped what has happened to them will be stunted or retarded in their growth into their eternal role as worshipers. How can those who profess faith in Christ ever be bored with worship? Boring worship is an oxymoron! How can those who come to worship—all the while eager for it to be finished so they can get on with their plans—understand their eternal role as worshipers? More importantly, perhaps, should the church so design its ministries as to accommodate the attention disorders of the average American shaped by a lifetime of watching thirty- and sixty minute television programs (with commercial interruptions)? Only a firm understanding of what the grace of God has accomplished in qualifying us to worship him—he brought the spiritually dead to life—will forever transform us as worshipers. Can people ever be qualified as, or ever want to be, worshipers of God if we never tell them of grace and the need for it?

If God is not absolutely holy, not just loving, and we are merely good people who have made the average few moral mistakes, then will we ever understand what it means that God has invited us to come boldly before the throne of grace?

PART  **3**

# RESTORING GOD
# TO THE CENTER
# OF WORSHIP

# THE ROLE OF WORSHIP IN THE CHURCH

Think about what a traditional church
is like. An old person greets you at the
door and hands you a mimeographed
bulletin. You sit in an uncomfortable
pew and stare at the back of someone's
head. You sing four-hundred-year-old-
songs and listen to a twenty-minute talk
about theology. Then they ask you for
money and kick you out.
—George Barna,
quoted in *Los Angeles Magazine*

## Observations of a Comet Watcher

As a seminary student in the middle of the 1970s, I was
involved actively in ministry at South Park Church, my home
church in suburban Chicago. There a young youth pastor
developed a pioneering ministry called "Son City." Frustrated
with the structures of an older established church, this young
man left with a number of youth to start a new church in a
movie theater. That church has traced a path like that of a
bright comet against the night sky. Willow Creek Commu-

131

nity Church and the "Willow Creek Model" are world-famous fifteen years later; and Bill Hybels is a Christian celebrity in great demand.

As a comet watcher I have often wondered why Willow Creek has had such a remarkable trajectory. Other churches have gifted and innovative people. To say "Bill was just at the right place at the right time" sounds like a bunch of sour grapes. To brand the ministry pure pragmatism is unfair and not at all accurate.

In the past couple years I have listened carefully to a number of tapes of the annual Willow Creek Pastors Conference. Much to my surprise, I have heard nothing remarkable on most of the tapes. Perhaps many of the insights don't sound revolutionary because so many of the principles have already been disseminated by others into the public domain. It was the simplest of the messages, by Bill himself, that seemed to hold the most arresting insight (I'll not say "the key") for understanding Willow Creek.

In a simple message, drawn from Acts 2 and from his memory of the origins of Willow Creek, Bill outlined the vision for the church that launched Willow Creek. Of all the things that Bill articulated in his folksy talk, he clearly distinguished and defined the various ministries of the church:

> worship
> making disciples
> evangelism

It appears that a key to the success of Willow Creek has been to carefully identify the purpose for each program or ministry of the church. Carefully defining and guarding the purpose for each ministry seems to be crucial to its success. The Sunday, and now Saturday, services are seeker services intended to evangelize non-Christians by building bridges to the kingdom of God in creative ways. These are not worship services, nor are they intended to be. The Thursday- (and now Wednesday-) night ministry is worship and is intended only for that purpose. The small-group ministries are designed to disciple believers into maturity.

I don't want to be unnecessarily simplistic, but I think this is crucial at a time when many churches appear to have lost sight of the clear purposes of the various traditional pro- grams of the church.

The worship service in some congregations is not worship at all. Instead, it is a part of a never-ending evangelistic tent meeting modeled after a Billy Graham crusade and moved into a permanent facility. Other services seem to be large- group discipleship classes with a song or two and, of course, an offering. Still others appear to be large-group psy- chotherapy sessions with two hymns and an offering. In many other churches we find a hybrid, the one-hour "let's worship, do evangelism, and build up the saints but don't forget to take the offering" service.

Perhaps the struggle of many churches today is rooted in the inevitable frustration and guaranteed ineffective- ness of trying to incorporate worship, evangelism, and dis- cipling all in one service a week. The pressure to do all three has prompted much of the pragmatism that disturbs some critics (including me). Having three services a week—Sunday morning, Sunday evening, and Wednesday evening—if they are all basically the same not only fails to address the problem but only adds to the obfuscation. We may call them worship services, Sunday-night fellow- ships, or mid-week services, but when they all have the same purpose, a poorly defined purpose, or the purpose of carrying on a tradition, we risk being ineffective in our ministries.

The traditional Sunday-night evangelistic service is now in decline, but it had a clear purpose at its inception. The Sunday-night service originated with the development of gas lighting. Churches discovered that non-Christians would attend an evening service in part because of the novelty of the new lighting. Making the evening service an evangelistic service was an appropriate response. But we have come a long way since then and the purpose of the Sunday-night service has been obscured.

It appears that Willow Creek has been successful, in part, because the purpose of each activity and ministry and program of the church is crisply differentiated and defined from Acts 2:42–47:

> They devoted themselves to the apostles' teaching and to the fellowship, to the breaking of bread and to prayer. Everyone was filled with awe, and many wonders and miraculous signs were done by the apostles. All the believers were together and had everything in common. Selling their possessions and goods, they gave to anyone as he had need. Every day they continued to meet together in the temple courts. They broke bread in their homes and ate together with glad and sincere hearts, praising God and enjoying the favor of all the people. And the Lord added to their number daily those who were being saved.

The church met for discipleship. They studied the teachings of the apostles and had small-group fellowship and prayer (v. 42).

The church worshiped regularly and shared the Lord's table together as the culmination of that regular practice of worship (v. 46).

The Jerusalem church also came together to evangelize, probably in the temple as on Pentecost. We are told the results in verse 47: they continued to add to their number.

One thing is clear. The ministry of the Jerusalem church—worship, discipleship (or nurture), and evangelism—was not accomplished on Sunday morning from 9:30 to 11:59. Each ministry of the church was individually targeted. Perhaps Robin Hood could hit two different targets shooting two arrows at the same time, but I doubt that the church can regularly hit two targets at once. And even Robin Hood could not hit three at the same time!

Many ministries of the church continue only because they are traditions. These ministries served a valid purpose when they were conceived (or were duplicated from other churches). Traditions are valid, proper, and healthy. God established traditions for his people, but these traditions serve to perpetuate a truth and a purpose. Traditions can be dangerous if we feel obligated to carry on ministries long after their purpose has been forgotten, fulfilled, or rendered obsolete.

The story may be apocryphal, but it has been reported that one church has in its minutes the following motion passed at a congregational meeting: "It was moved and seconded and approved that we continue to do what we have always done, whatever that is." We must take heed of the maxim: "Whoever aims at nothing is certain to hit it every time."

Simplistic though this analysis may be, Willow Creek reminds us of the importance of keeping the purposes and goals of our ministries clearly defined and articulated for all.

## Integrating Worship, Evangelism, and Discipleship

Worship, making disciples, and evangelism, the three distinct functions of the church, are closely connected and interdependent (see illustration 8.1).

Recruiting worshipers, the task we generally call evangelism, is one of the essential ministries of the church. It is

**Illustration 8.1**
*The Ministries of the Church*
(Acts 2:42–47)

## Evangelism

Every day they continued to meet together in the temple courts . . .

[E]njoying the favor of all the people . . .

And the Lord added to their number daily those who were being saved.

## Worship

they devoted themselves to the . . . breaking of bread. . . .

They broke bread in their homes and ate together with glad and sincere hearts, praising God. . . .

## Discipleship

They devoted themselves to the apostles' teaching and to the fellowship, to the breaking of bread and to prayer.

God who is seeking worshipers: "Yet a time is coming and has now come when the true worshipers will worship the Father in spirit and truth, for they are *the kind of worshipers the Father seeks*" (John 4:23, italics added). The evangelistic ministry of the church is intimately related to the ministry of worship. God has called us to worship him, and a natural expression of that worship is to make his name known so that others will worship the true God also. From the time God called Abraham, his purpose for calling a people has been the same—to glorify God in the earth by making his name great.

The missionary mandate of Israel as the people of God is found clearly stated in worshipful passages like Psalm 67:

> May God be gracious to us and bless us
> and make his face shine upon us,
> that your ways may be known on earth,
> your salvation among all nations.
> May the peoples praise you, O God;
> May all the peoples praise you.
> May the nations be glad and sing for joy,
> for you rule the peoples justly
> and guide the nations of the earth.
> May the peoples praise you, O God,
> may the peoples praise you.
> Then the land will yield its harvest,
> and God, our God, will bless us.
> God will bless us,
> and all the ends of the earth will fear him.

That all the nations and peoples might bless YHWH, the God of the Israelites, the true God, is the desire of the psalmist.[1] Calling all people to forsake their false gods and worship the right God is the task of God's people. God called Israel to worship him and to be a conduit for others to worship him also.

The Great Commission, repeated in five distinct expressions in the New Testament (once each in the four Gospels and once in Acts)[2], is neither a surprise nor a revisionist tactic. We could, it seems, call it the great recommissioning of God's people in the era of the church. The announcement of the universal scope of the gospel was accompanied by the investiture of the Holy Spirit, who indwells each believer with power. The promise of power from the Holy Spirit for the fulfillment of the Great Commission may be new for the church age, but the Great Commission itself is not.

This is the essence of Paul's evangelistic plea on Mars Hill: "For as I walked around and looked carefully at your objects of worship, I even found an altar with this inscription: TO AN UNKNOWN GOD. Now what you worship as unknown I am going to proclaim to you" (Acts 17:23). Paul's message expresses God's desire that all people know him, that all nations know his name. "God did this so that men would seek him and perhaps reach out for him and find him, though he is not far from each one of us. 'For in him we live and move and have our being'" (Acts 17:27–28). The apostle desired to make known among the Gentiles the true God he himself had encountered.

God's program of calling people to give up worshiping the wrong gods and to worship the true God is most clearly exemplified in Paul's description of the Christians at Thessalonica:

> Therefore we do not need to say anything about it, for they themselves report what kind of reception you gave us. They tell how you *turned to God from idols to serve the living and true God,* and to wait for his Son from heaven, whom he raised from the dead—Jesus, who rescues us from the coming wrath. [1 Thess. 1:8b–10, italics added]

We see again the close relationship between worship and evangelism: evangelism is the task of recruiting others to turn from worshiping false gods and to worship the true God.

It is fitting that those who have met the true and living God should announce to those who worship false gods or dead gods that the true and living God can be found, can be known, and is worthy of worship.

Evangelism and worship are related in another way as well. Worship supplies the proper motivation for the task of global evangelization. Worship was, of course, the impetus for the commissioning of Isaiah. He responded to the call of the holy God whom he saw the exalted in the temple: "Here am I. Send me!" God found among his worshipers a man who would go and proclaim his word. Gerrit Gustafson rightly observes that when worship is seperated from evangelism, worship can degenerate into the ongoing pursuit of a spiritual high. Conversely, when evangelism is separated from worship it becomes bound up in duty and guilt.[3]

A quarter of a century ago, John Stott identified four reasons for the reluctance of contemporary Christians to witness. Chief among these was the lack of a compelling motivation.[4] If evangelical Christians lack a compelling motivation for evangelism, it is proper that we should ask "Why?" If we can take any wisdom at all from the ministry of Isaiah, we could easily speculate that what is missing when Christians are not motivated to evangelism is a life-changing encounter with God in worship.

Worship and evangelism are inseparable ministries of the church. The church exists to worship and to call others to worship as well. If the church is not effective in its witness, the diagnostic chart might well indicate that people are not truly entering into worship—life-changing worship—in the presence of God.

Making disciples, the training and nurture of the people of God, is the second vital ministry of the church. Like worship and evangelism, it does not stand alone. We see this clearly if we return to 1 Thessalonians 1:4–8:

For we know, brothers loved by God, that he has chosen you, because our gospel came to you not simply with words, but also with power, with the Holy Sprit and with deep conviction. You know how we lived among you for your sake. You became imitators of us and of the Lord; in spite of severe suffering, you welcomed the message with the joy given by the Holy Spirit. And so you became a model to all the believers in Macedonia and in Achaia. The Lord's message rang out from you not only in Macedonia and Achaia—your faith in God has become known everywhere.

There emerges a clear pattern for the church and its ministry of making disciples of all nations.

First, we note the conversion of the Thessalonians. They turned to God from their idols in response to the message and the power of the Holy Spirit.

Second, we see the imitation of the Thessalonians. They copied the life of Paul, and through Paul the Lord Jesus. This is the essence of disciple making—the life of a disciple stamped or imprinted into the life of another. Paul uses a Greek word from which we get the English "mimic" and "mimeograph." It means to make a copy, a duplicate.

Third, we observe that the Thessalonians became witnesses of the Lord throughout Asia Minor. Having turned to God, they in turn recruited others to come and worship the true God whom they had encountered through the message of the gospel. The pattern is simple (see illustration 8.2).

The process of making disciples is cyclical. It begins with evangelization, then comes 360 degrees as converts evangelize still others because they have become copies of those who ministered to them.

**Conviction→ Conversion→ Imitation→ Evangelization**

## Illustration 8.2
### *Making Disciples*

| Conversion | Imitation | Modeling |
|---|---|---|

| 1 Thess. 1:5 | 1 Thess. 1:6 | 1 Thess. 1:7 |
|---|---|---|
| Because our gospel came to you not simply with words, but also with power, with the Holy Spirit and with deep conviction. | You became imitators of us and of the Lord; in spite of severe suffering you welcomed the message with the joy given by the Holy Spirit. | And so you became a model to all the believers in Macedonia and Achaia. |

**1 Thess. 1:9**

They tell how you turned to God from idols to serve the living and true God.

The process of world evangelization depends upon this process of multiplicative disciple making.

As I implied earlier, the process of making disciples is critical to the church's call to worship the Lord. It is only the process of discipleship that will turn anyone who comes to the church on their terms into servants "who no longer live for themselves, but for him." If we never effectively disciple our converts, we will continue to import the world's values into the church and will continue to be squeezed into the world's mold. Only by making disciples out of new believers will we cause them to shed not only the world's values but also the world's methods. Only when we have discipled new belivers can we expect them to abandon any pragmatic methodolgies and embrace the truth of 2 Corinthians 10:3–4: "For though we live in the world, we do not wage war as the world does. The weapons we fight with are not the weapons of the world. On the contrary, they have divine power to demolish strongholds."

A comprehensive discipleship program must rightly emphasize several areas: how to read and study the Bible, how to pray, how to witness, how to gain victory over sin, how to discover your spiritual gift. We see the relationships in illustration 8.3.

What is missing, however, is one important link. When we disciple converts we must also emphasize training and teaching young believers to worship even as we equip them to witness and to serve. There are many fine books on discipleship and on worship. There appears to be a need for materials and programs focused on training Christians to worship as a primary objective of discipleship. Have we succumbed to the notion that worship is adequately learned by osmosis?

We seem to have in the church an abundance of seminars, Sunday-school classes, support groups, Bible studies dealing with subjects from Christian financial management to coping with dysfunctional families. These are badly needed, but not at the cost of neglecting our primary calling as worshipers. Because our highest calling is not to stewardship or to marriage but to worship, we must provide deliberate, systematic instruction in worship as a part of the process of making disciples.

**Illustration 8.3**
*The Ministries of the Church Put in Motion*

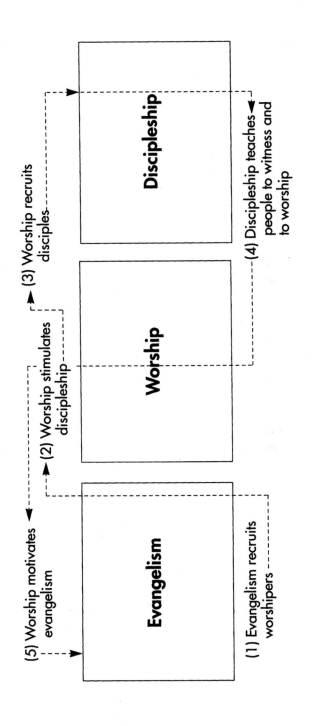

Understanding the interconnection of worship with evangelism and disciple making is important if the church is to accomplish effectively all three tasks. But while we need to see the interconnectedness of these areas of ministry, we need to guard against a spiritual stew where none of the individual ingredients can be distinguished. Unlike Willow Creek, many churches seem to have lost the clear distinction between worship, evangelism, and discipleship. If we are to be effective worshipers, disciplers, and evangelists, we must be intentional in our ministries.

Worship, then, is not only the third major ministry of the church, but also the logical center of all the ministries of the church. Worship—the central activity of heaven and the purpose for which we were created—is the central purpose of the church. The church together in worship is its most visible expression. Although this centrality of worship is proper, we must not let ourselves be deceived by the common misconception that the church gathered for worship is the sum of the church or its ministry. On a practical level, worship is the center of the life of the church because it is the most visible event in the life of the church. Because worship is at the hub of what we do in the church, we need to make certain that it is fastened securely to the axle of biblical truth that turns it.

# THE FOCUS OF THE WORSHIP SERVICE

What nerve you Christians have using
a word like "service" (a word filled with
blood, sweat and tears) to denote your
sedate gatherings at which you sit and
think and sometimes only sit.
—attributed
to John Ruskin

One does not need to visit many Protestant American
churches to find one that reveals muddled purposes. If you
had visited either of the churches I pastored for the first
years of my ministry you would have quickly discovered one.
I certainly didn't know any better; seminary never dealt with
worship in a practical way. A sample order of service from a
bulletin I picked up recently reveals what I mean:

---

**Prelude**

**Hymn: Come, Christians, Join to Sing**

**Invocation**

**Greet One Another**

**News of the Church**

Missions Report

Offering

Anthem: O God Our Help in Ages Past [Arr.: Thompson]

Pastoral Prayer

Scripture Reading

Hymn: I'm So Glad to Be Part of the Family of God

Solo

Message: God's Plan for the Family

Hymn: Trust and Obey

Invitation

---

This service may have been called a worship service, but it really was an attempt to worship, to evangelize, and to build the body in one hour. The worshiper was primarily a spectator, not a participant. The drama of worship was missing. The focus again and again turned from God to the worshipers themselves.

Granted, some churches have two- and three-hour services on Sunday that incorporate all manner of ministries, but these tend to be the exception. Our television-oriented culture appears to have a fifty-nine-minute attention span that seems to dictate our ministry. If the culture limits us to one hour, let us make certain we use that hour for one thing: worship! If the church is to be revitalized and to turn around the trend of decline, there can be no better place to start than by setting aside one hour a week when all we do is worship and praise God. Let the focus be on God. Let everything else be put aside. Let every moment of the hour be committed to that one supreme task.

As we look at the church we see two important areas where the problems of integrating worship, discipleship, and evangelism surface. The first is the area of music, a province of the church that stirs great controversy and strong feelings. This is no recent phenomenon, however, for we are told that even Spurgeon referred to the music department as the "War Department." The second area is preaching. If we can borrow again from Spurgeon we might begin to see the issue. Spurgeon suggested that he preached one-third for the sinners and two-thirds for the saints. I have long appreciated that advice as sound, but I have wondered how that fits with the church's three ministries: worship, disciple making, and evangelism.

Perhaps we can better accomplish our purposes in the church if we apply these categories to the two important areas of music and preaching.

## Sharpening Our Focus on Music

The music we use in the church often suggests ambiguity or misunderstanding about worship. Music appreciation is quite subjective, so there is little value in suggesting here what constitutes good music. That is not my concern. The elements of music (harmony, key, chord structures) are important but secondary. There is good music and bad music in every category and from every era in the church: classics, spirituals, traditional, hymns, gospel songs, choruses, praise songs, Scripture songs, and the Psalter. In each era there are styles and trends, but each era seems to leave behind a few outstanding additions to our lasting lexicon of church music.

What makes church music "good"? It may be a circular argument, but what the church uses and preserves and perpetuates over a period of years is usually good. Usually, but not always, this means music that is technically solid, melodies that can be sung by congregations, meaningful lyrics, and words that fit the music.

As we evaluate church music, it is vital to keep in mind that perhaps no issue is as divisive as what kind of music should be utilized. At times the debate seems not only confusing but silly. Some might argue that contemporary music is unfit because there is so much repetition of just a few words and not much message. Others counter that Handel's *Messiah* includes nearly one hundred repetitions of "Hallelujah!" Some argue that percussion instruments are inappropriate for worship (and even talk about the sensual nature of rhythm), but then turn a deaf ear to Psalm 150: "Praise [the LORD] with tambourine and dancing."

The debate over church music most often focuses on subjective matters of taste; and on those matters the Scriptures are silent. We do not know what the Old Testament tunes were. No one has the music to Psalms 82 through 90. We don't know the tune of "Gittith." We do not know the melody of the Songs of Ascent (Pss. 120–134). We don't know the songs of the Hallel that Jesus sang with his disciples to close the Last Supper. The church has not made recordings of the songs Paul and Silas rehearsed at midnight to take advantage of the acoustics of the Philippian jail. We don't know what "hymns and spiritual songs" were sung in Corinth. Church history has not preserved a record of the "hymns to Christ as God" that prompted Pliny to mention them in correspondence with Emperor Trajan.

All of this is to suggest that arguing about church music is subjective. Many of the debates accomplish nothing, and are reminiscent of Dick Clark having a panel of young people rate a new release on "American Bandstand": "I liked it, it's easy to worship to, so I give it a 90." What we like dominates the debate.

More important, Scripture does not prescribe a style of music. The Holy Spirit has used and continues to use many styles and expressions of music, from Gregorian chants to Christian rap, to bring glory to the Father. Consequently, for a person to argue for any particular style as the "right" style of music borders on idolatry, as Paul Westermeyer correctly observes in *The Christian Century*.[1]

Since we cannot resolve the debate over church music, perhaps we can at least elevate the debate to a more objective level. To do that we can employ a set of questions that seek to transcend matters of taste. The questions will help us evaluate music in terms of its utility: how does a piece of music serve the purpose of worship in a particular place at a particular time? We can ask several diagnostic questions about any piece of music we might be considering for worship.

*Is this a song of worship, nurture, or evangelism?* We need first to look at the music of the church in terms of its focus and purpose. Three general categories relate to the three ministries of the church: worship music, nurturant music, and evangelistic music. This simple classification helps us to see how much of our Christian music is related not to worship but to evangelism or to building up the body of Christ. Some music may fit into more than one category. So, although it may be impossible to fit every piece of music neatly into the grid, the exercise of classification is valuable because it reveals a basic characteristic we should seek to discover about every piece of music we use in worship.

It may be helpful to demonstrate this by categorizing a number of sample selections.

### Illustrations 9.1
*Categories of Music for the Church*

| Worship Music (Sung to God) | Nurturant Music (Sung to the body) | Evangelistic Music (Sung to the church, including unbelievers) |
|---|---|---|
| Great Is Thy Faithfulness | We've a Story to Tell to the Nations | Living for Jesus |

| Worship Music | Nurturant Music | Evangelistic Music |
|---|---|---|
| We Sing the Mighty Power of God | I Am His and He Is Mine | Who Is on the Lord's Side |
| I Love You Lord | Love Lifted Me | Just As I Am |
| We Praise Thee, O God | All That Thrills My Soul Is Jesus | Stand Up, Stand Up for Jesus |
| O Lord, You're Beautiful | A Song for the Nations | What a Friend We Have in Jesus |
| My Jesus, I Love Thee | Now I Belong to Jesus | There's Room at the Cross for You |
| Glorify Thy Name in All the Earth | Jesus, Jesus, Jesus | Softly and Tenderly |
| He Is Lord | He Has Made Me Glad | At the Cross |
| Thank You Lord | Nothing But the Blood | At Calvary |
| There Is a Redeemer | Come, Christians, Join to Sing | Jesus Calls Us o'er the Tumult |
| All Hail King Jesus | Amazing Grace | Jesus Saves! |
| Holy, Holy, Holy | Let Your Heart Be Broken | |
| We Will Glorify | Be Still, My Soul | |

When the category is not clear, some secondary questions may help:

What is the overall purpose of the song?
Is it about God?
Is it about how I feel?
Is it exhortation—about what others should do?
Is it a prayer to God?

*To whom is this song sung?* Much of what we sing in the church is sung to each other rather than to God! If we exclude hymns of praise that are about God but are not actually addressed to God (e.g., "A Mighty Fortress"), we are still left with an abundance of "horizontal" music.

But let us understand that many of these songs (i.e., "Love Lifted Me") are not pure songs of worship because their focus is on ourselves and how we feel. Many of these are the "old favorite" gospel songs of the 1860–1940 era—a narrow span of church history. We tend to sing them to one another rather than to God himself, so we must be careful how we use these songs. The danger is that many of the songs in many hymnals today "tend," according to David Fisher, "in the direction of glorifying Christian experience."[2] There is clearly a place for horizontal music in the church, and we find that these songs are most often appropriately songs of response to God, especially in response to the preaching of God's Word.

*How does this piece of music relate to our affections?* Music has the capacity to generate, express, and inspire affections. When we select music, we need to identify, when possible, how the music relates to our affections. Too often we may look to music to generate feelings that are not otherwise there.

*What role does or should this song have in the drama of worship?* If we understand the dramatic nature of worship and to whom a song is addressed we can better select music for the role that it plays in worship.

With a dramatic view of worship we see each event generally as either in an *impressive* event (God speaks to us) or an *expressive* event (we respond to God). For example, an anthem, a solo, a Scripture reading, a drama, or a sermon may be impressive events. Congregational singing, prayer, and quiet meditation are primarily expressive events in the drama.

Perhaps part of our confusion is that music can serve as either an impressive or expressive event in worship depending on its place, its purpose, and its audience. An anthem may be an impressive event communicating the greatness of God. It may, then, inspire a response of praise expressed through a congregational song, a prayer, or even silence. Some music selections, like the spiritual "Were You There?" were written to generate affections. Other songs are prayers of commitment sung to God and express our affections. Each piece of music should be evaluated in terms of its place, who will sing it, and to whom it will be sung.

*Are the lyrics clear, correct, and appropriate for those singing or listening?* I think that most Christians would veto "Drop Kick Me, Jesus, Through the Goal Posts of Life" as inappropriate. But what should we do with "There Is a Balm in Gilead" in an age when even most Christians know little about Gilead and nothing about balm? This and many other hymns were written in a poetic style that renders them obscure or incomprehensible. The unchurched person finds them irrelevant.

It is not inappropriate to add to or change words to make them more fitting for the church. Hymns are not sacred Scripture, and translations of Scripture are not either, so we may modernize seventeenth-century English whenever it is obscure.

Much of the debate over music could be avoided if we could first perform this simple five-step diagnostic for each piece of music selected for our worship. There is a place for all three kinds of music in the church.

Clearly, the what-we-like trap has ensnared many churches that categorically reject almost anything with a Maranatha or a Hosanna logo. They may have room only for the Singspiration logo. This attitude is an expression of our self-centeredness.

Make no mistake, however. It is not just a problem for those who like the old hymns, traditional gospel songs, or even the classics. Too many churches that have opted for contemporary music suffer from a single-criteria selection process of their own. Consequently, many church members are being cut off from a wide range of great music of the past. A rock radio station in Los Angeles advertises that it plays "No music by dead guys!" People in the contemporary church are being cheated by a similar unfortunate attitude.

What I find most interesting is to view the trends in Christian music in this century. The period of 1900–1940 gave us many gospel songs from Percy Crawford, Fanny Crosby, and others. Yet so many of these gospel songs are self-centered and deal with how we feel rather than with who God is. These songs contrast starkly to the trend of contemporary music, much of which is sung to God as an offering of praise. What is surprising is that we should expect the reverse pattern. As the existentialism of the century continues to affect the church, the worship music being written today generally turns away from the "I/me" music of the first half of the century.

Our music is destined to be self-centered if our primary criterion for selecting music is what we like. Our debate over music has polarized and split many churches. It is a manifestation of self-centeredness creeping into our worship.

## Shaping Our Forms for Preaching

Donald Macleod of Princeton Seminary wrote: "It is alarming to note how the function of the preacher and the purpose of his preaching have become blurred in the thinking of not a few contemporary congregations."[3] If that observation were valid thirty years ago, it is much more valid today. That blurred vision appears to be the product of our traditional approach to preaching. The abundance of preaching today seems to fall into two categories. First, there is a great deal of discipleship or nurturant preaching for the saints. This kind of preaching concentrates on issues of Christian life and doctrine; texts and teaching usually come from the Pauline epistles. Second, there is evangelistic preaching, which in some circles is dominant.

If we think again of the three primary ministries of the church—worship, discipleship, and evangelism—we must wonder why only two kinds of preaching dominate. Preaching most often takes place in a worship service, but rarely does the preaching relate to the context itself—worship. Robert Bailey writes: "At the outset we must restore the thrust of God-centered worship. . . . There must be some corrective course of action whereby a tenable proposal for a union of preaching and worship could be achieved."[4] I would make such a tenable proposal by arguing for a third category: worship preaching. Worship preaching is theological preaching that focuses on God, his character, his attributes, his person, his acts, and his glory. Worship is not always strictly practical and relevant. In fact, practicality and relevance are at times obstacles to worship because they maintain our focus on the things of this world rather than on the eternal kingdom.

Worship preaching will not always be strictly relevant to this world because we do not belong to this world! Our obsession with relevance and practicality at times borders on idolatry. Worship preaching needs to focus on declaring who

God is. Borrowing from *Willmington's Book of Bible Lists,*
we could outline a sample preaching calendar for six months
that deals with who God is:[5]

| | | |
|---|---|---|
| 1. | God is self-existing | Exodus 3:13–14 |
| 2. | God is self-sufficient | Psalm 50:1–12 |
| 3. | God is eternal | Deuteronomy 33:27; Psalm 90 |
| 4. | God is infinite | 1 Kings 8:22–27 |
| 5. | God is omnipresent | Psalm 139:7–12 |
| 6. | God is omniscient | Psalm 139:2–6 |
| 7. | God is omnipotent | Genesis 18 |
| 8. | God is wise | Proverbs 3 |
| 9. | God is immutable | Hebrews 1:10–12; 13:8 |
| 10. | God is sovereign | Isaiah 46:9–11 |
| 11. | God is incomprehensible | Job 11:7–19 |
| 12. | God is holy | Isaiah 6 |
| 13. | God is righteous and just | Psalm 119:137 |
| 14. | God is true | John 17:3 |
| 15. | God is faithful | Psalm 89:1–2 |
| 16. | God is light | James 1:17 |
| 17. | God is good | Psalm 107:8 |
| 18. | God is merciful | Psalm 103:8–17 |
| 19. | God is gracious | Psalm 111:4 |
| 20. | God is love | Romans 5:8 |
| 21. | God is spirit | John 4:24 |
| 22. | God is one | Deuteronomy 6:4–5 |
| 23. | God is triune | Matthew 28:19 |

Perhaps wisdom dictates that we not preach a series of
twenty-three messages on any subject, but certainly a short
series on the character of God should be a welcome part of
worship. Perhaps we are afraid that worship preaching on
who God is might not be pleasing to the saints who, in our
age of human-centered Christianity, demand that messages
always be relevant and practical.

A decade ago I preached a ten-part series on the names of God. I found the study rich, and I thought the messages were solid. That not everyone was pleased became painfully evident. Because the messages didn't contain the usual number of stories and illustrations or were not immediately practical, I took heat from an otherwise very supportive congregation. I was redeemed recently when my foremost critic called from the East Coast. He told me that from a new perspective, these messages had been the most beneficial from among the hundreds of messages he had heard me preach.

I think it was Ben Patterson of the *Wittenburg Door* who first referred to the great temptation of preaching as "turning bread into stones." We know the Word of God is the bread of life, but we are tempted to believe that the Word of God is dull, boring, and powerless until we transform it into bread by our great preaching. The temptation is to think that the power of the Word of God is in our ability to make it edible!

One aspect of this temptation is the temptation of practicality or relevancy. We who preach think that it is our primary job to make the Bible practical. Truth for its own sake, we are deceived into thinking, is not sufficient either to nurture God's people, to hold an audience, or to attract the unchurched. It leads to "how-to" sermons and cookbook-style preaching where there is little emphasis on concept and much emphasis on application. A quick glance at the church page in any major newspaper reveals a host of sermon titles that sound more like recipes than like sermons to promote worship. When Kathleen Neumeyer examined one market-driven church for her secular article, "God for Sale," she noted the same phenomenon: "[The sermon titles] sound like titles from the self-help section of Waldenbooks."[6]

The church today has little interest in theology, prompting Martin Marty to conclude that "the faith of many Americans is a vague, oblong blur."[7] We act like schoolchildren

in math class who are more interested looking in the back
of the book for the answers to the problems than in understanding the mathematical principles behind the answers.
Under the umbrella of the whole counsel of God come
"God's Plan for Your Needs," "How to Cope with Stress,"
"How to Discipline Children."
These are all biblical topics and all are needed in the body
of Christ. These may even be great subjects for drawing non-
Christians into the church. But with preaching that continually addresses felt needs, American Christians risk
remaining theologically shallow and ignorant. Moreover, the
emphasis on human-centered preaching will continue to fil-
ter into our worship when we have not carefully established
the singular and primary purpose of worship. The question
we must ask, then, is, "Does this message facilitate worship
of God or does it reinforce our focus on ourselves as the ultimate reality?"

The preaching reported in Nehemiah serves as a biblical
model for worship preaching. The people of God assembled
to hear God speak to them:

> . . . Ezra the priest brought the Law before the assembly,
> which was made up of men and women and all who were
> able to understand. . . .
> Ezra the scribe stood on a high wooden platform built for
> the occasion. . . .
> Ezra opened the book . . . and as he opened it, the
> people all stood up. Ezra praised the LORD, the great God;
> and all the people lifted their hands and responded, "Amen!
> Amen!" Then they bowed down and worshiped the Lord with
> their faces to the ground.
> The Levites . . . instructed the people in the Law while
> the people were standing there. They read from the Book of
> the Law of God, making it clear and giving the meaning so
> that the people could understand what was being read. [Neh.
> 8:2, 4–8]

The reading and teaching from the Word of God stimulated responsive worship of God. The reading of the Word prompted a range of responses. The people of God wept. The people of God grieved. The people obeyed the Word of God, building booths for the Feast of Tabernacles that was called for during the seventh month. These were genuine responses of worship—responses to hearing the Word and the name of the Lord proclaimed.

We must see a distinct genre of worship preaching if we are going to revive worship. Developing worship preaching as a category of preaching is not something that can proceed without some tension in the church. The pressure toward so-called relevance and practicality as supremely important reflects how our age has influenced even our worship. The debate in many churches over music likes and dislikes is a manifestation of the same self-centeredness. When we make demands, spoken or unspoken, about preaching or music or worship in general, we are approaching God with our agenda, not his. Our demands or our complaining about preaching or music dishonor the God we claim to worship. We will continue to struggle with these pressures until we come to grips with the sacrificial nature of worship and let go of our own agendas.

# THE HIGH COST OF WORSHIP

10

... most seemed concerned with how
to get more out of the Christian life. I
wanted to know how to put more into it.
—Chuck Colson,
*Loving God*

## The Personal Nature of Worship

The difference between bacon and eggs, we are told in a homespun one-liner, is that while the chicken may be actively involved, the pig is committed. This may not be a great theological truth, but in a rather simple way it points us toward an important aspect of worship. Many people may be involved casually in worship, but real worship exacts the price of commitment that is altogether different. Worship requires not just personal involvement but personal sacrifice.

Throughout the pages of God's Word we find an important chain of statements about the personal nature of worship. True worship cannot be casual or incidental. Tokenism is not true worship, as Hosea reminded the people of God:

> For I desire mercy, not sacrifice,
>    and acknowledgment of God rather than burnt offerings.
> [Hos. 6:6]

Isaiah was even more emphatic as he pronounced the oracle of God to his people:

> "The multitude of your sacrifices—
>    what are they to me?" says the LORD.
> "I have more than enough burnt offerings,
>    of rams and the fat of fattened animals;
> I have no pleasure
>    in the blood of bulls and lambs and goats. . . .
> Your incense is detestable to me. . . .
> Your New Moon festivals and your appointed feasts
>    my soul hates." [1:11, 13, 14]

Token worship is offensive to God because he is a personal God who is concerned with essential matters of the heart and of our relationship to him. It has always been that way, and we need to remember that in this age of human-centered Christianity.

## The Personal God

It is a personal God who calls us to worship him:

> [A]scribe to the LORD the glory due his name.
> Bring an offering and come before him;
>    worship the LORD in the splendor of his holiness.
> [1 Chron. 16:29]

> Worship the LORD in the splendor of his holiness;
>    tremble before him, all the earth. [Ps. 96:9]

The holy, eternal God has called us again and again to worship him. He has commanded that we worship no other.

There is for God's earth-bound creation a paradox of being called by an unseen God to worship him. He has made us to live in a material world yet calls us to worship himself, the God who transcends the material world. He calls us to worship by faith, believing that the unseen kingdom and the unseen King are as real and more permanent than the sensory world we live in.

Many will not worship by faith and will instead put false gods before the true God. These are often material and tangible gods who do not transcend the created world. The natural human part of us wants a god that is immanent—present here with us and discerned by our senses—but also bigger than us. We want our gods to be transcendent and immanent at the same time.

Paul reminded the pantheists of Athens that the unknown and true God is transcendent but also immanent: "He is not far from each one of us. 'For in him we live and move and have our being'" (Acts 17:27–28). He is transcendent, but he is not remote. Nor do we worship someone who is simply not there.

The immanence of God is made clear from the earliest chapters of the Bible. God walked with Adam in the garden. God met with Abraham when the three visitors, one of whom was YHWH, appeared to Abraham:

> When the men got up to leave, they looked down toward Sodom, and Abraham walked along with them to see them on their way. Then the LORD said, "Shall I hide from Abraham what I am about to do?" . . .
> Then the LORD said, "The outcry against Sodom and Gomorrah is so great and their sin so grievous that I will go down and see if what they have done is as bad as the outcry that has reached me. If not, I will know."
> The men turned away and went toward Sodom, but Abraham remained standing before the LORD. Then Abraham approached him and said: "Will you sweep away the right-

eous with the wicked? What if there are fifty righteous people in the city? Will you really sweep it away and not spare
the place for the sake of the fifty righteous people in it? Far
be it from you to do such a thing—to kill the righteous with
the wicked, treating the righteous and the wicked alike. Far
be it from you! Will not the Judge of all the earth do right?"
[Gen. 18:16–17, 20–25]

This is a remarkable text. It is usually translated according to the Masoretic text: "Abraham remained standing in
front of the LORD." This is not the actual Hebrew text, however, as the textual footnote in the New International Version indicates. In what appears to be the only verse in all of
the Old Testament Masoretic text deliberately changed from
the original Hebrew, the Hebrew reads: "the LORD remained
standing before Abraham." The Masoretes apparently could
not accept the idea that God would stand before Abraham
and amended the text. It appears, however, that "the LORD
remained standing" in front of Abraham to prompt Abraham
to intercede for Sodom![1]

God's immanence is crucial for our ability to worship him.
The transcendent One who called us to worship him is himself immanent! He is near to each one of us! He is both transcendent and immanent. Perhaps it is because God is a person that he can without contradiction be both immanent
and transcendent.

God is a person and he made us as persons in his likeness. Because we are persons and he is a personal God, we
have the capacity to worship him and to know him and to
love him.

Moses was confronted at the burning bush by the God
who is both immanent and transcendent:

"Do not come any closer," God said. "Take off your san-
dals, for the place where you are standing is holy ground."
Then he said, "I am the God of your father, the God of Abra-

ham, the God of Isaac and the God of Jacob." At this, Moses
hid his face, because he was afraid to look at God. . . . "So I
have come down to rescue them from the hand of the Egyptians and to bring them up out of that land into a good and
spacious land, . . . I will be with you. And this will be the
sign to you that it is I who have sent you: When you have
brought the people out of Egypt, you will worship God on
this mountain." . . .
    God said to Moses, "I AM WHO I AM. This is what you are
to say to the Israelites: 'I AM has sent me to you.'"
    God also said to Moses, "Say to the Israelites, 'The LORD,
the God of your fathers—the God of Abraham, the God of
Isaac and the God of Jacob—has sent me to you.' This is my
name forever, the name by which I am to be remembered
from generation to generation." [Exod. 3:5–15]

Only to Moses did God reveal a name by which he may be
called by those who know him. YHWH is a name unlike any
other—that is to be expected. It is a personal name, for he
desires not only to be worshiped but also to be known in
relationship with the persons he created. To the nations he
is Elohim, the God of creation. To Abraham and Isaac and
Jacob he revealed himself as El Shaddai, God Almighty, but
not as YHWH, the LORD (see Exod. 6:2–3).

The relational God, YHWH, who reveals himself as a person, promises immanence and relationship with his people.
The three-part promise he made to Israel is restated in his
eternal kingdom.

  1. He will be their God.
  2. They will be his people.
  3. He will dwell with them.

This first promise appears in Genesis 17:8: "I will be their
God." In Exodus 6:7 the second provision is added to the
announcement: "I will take you as my own people, and I will
be your God." In Exodus 29:45 the formula is completed

with the third proclamation: "Then I will dwell among the Israelites and be their God." This three-part formula runs through the Old Testament in various expressions. It is the heart of the new covenant announced in Jeremiah 31 and quoted in Hebrews 8:8–12. It is confirmed again in 2 Corinthians 6:16 and is realized in Revelation 21:3: "Now the dwelling of God is with men, and he will live with them. They will be his people, and God himself will be with them and be their God."

The God who calls us to worship him is the holy, transcendent Creator. But from the beginning to the end of his written revelation, he underscores that he is a personal God who pitches his tent with us for all eternity. He is the God who dwells with his people—in the cloud of the shekinah glory, in the incarnation of Christ, in the indwelling of the Holy Spirit, and ultimately in the kingdom.

## The Personal Nature of Appropriate Sacrifices

In other times and other traditions, people presented inanimate offerings to inanimate idols. A living God, however, should be worshiped with living offerings. Because our God is personal and relational, our worship of him must gravitate away from offerings of lifeless things and toward personal expressions of worship. Sacrifices from God's people can take many forms. The Word provides some clear instruction:

> Through Jesus, therefore, let us continually offer to God a sacrifice of praise—the fruit of lips that confess his name. [Heb. 13:15]

> The sacrifices of God are a broken spirit;
> a broken and contrite heart,
> O God, you will not despise. [Ps. 51:17]

> To do what is right and just
> is more acceptable to the LORD than sacrifice. [Prov. 21:3]

For I desire mercy, not sacrifice,
and acknowledgment rather than burnt offerings.
[Hos. 6:6]

Throughout the Scriptures we are confronted with this prescription: the immaterial God desires immaterial offerings, not material ones.

## The Nature of Sacrifice

As we noted in chapter 3, there can be no doubt from Scripture that while salvation is free, worship is costly. To worship is to ascribe worth, to declare by our sacrifice that God is worthy! Mary, when she used the occasion of a dinner party to honor Jesus with an expensive gift of ointment, declared that Jesus was worthy of such an offering. She entered into "worth-ship."

Sacrifice is not a popular word in our culture. Most Christians, including myself, know little of what sacrifice is. Most of what we know we know by having seen or heard about others who sacrificed for the kingdom of God. When we read in Hebrews 11 about those who were sawed in two, went about in sheepskins, or were tortured, stoned, destitute, persecuted, and mistreated, we wonder how we would respond in similar times of testing. For many of us sacrifice means giving up a convenience or a privilege. We have rarely dug much deeper.

King David understood that for worship to be genuine, it must be rooted in sacrifice:

> On that day Gad went to David and said to him, "Go up and build an altar to the LORD on the threshing floor of Araunah the Jebusite. . . . "O king, Araunah gives all this to the king." Araunah also said to him, "May the LORD your God accept you."

> But the king replied to Araunah, "No, I insist on paying you for it. I will not sacrifice to the LORD my God burnt offerings that cost me nothing."
>
> So David bought the threshing floor and the oxen and paid fifty shekels of silver for them. David built an altar to the LORD there and sacrificed burnt offerings and fellowship offerings. [2 Sam. 24:18, 23–25]

David acknowledged that an offering, whether an ox or a sacrifice of praise, was empty if another provided. It then was of diminished worth.

### *Living Sacrifices*

God has no need of animal sacrifices. The sacrifice of worship that God desires is, in essence, a sacrifice of self. This is the essence of Paul's argument in Romans 12:1–2:

> Therefore, I urge you, brothers, in view of God's mercy, to offer your bodies as living sacrifices, holy and pleasing to God—this is your spiritual act of worship. Do not conform any longer to the pattern of this world, but be transformed by the renewing of your mind. Then you will be able to test and approve what God's will is—his good, pleasing and perfect will.

A living sacrifice—an obedient life lived—is a reasonable offering for those who "no longer live for themselves but for him who died for them and was raised again" (2 Cor. 5:15).

Paul argues that this is a reasonable sacrifice for us to make in light of the mercies of God. When Paul suggested this in Romans 12, he was building upon all that he had laid out in the first eleven chapters:

Rom. 1: the sinfulness and lostness of man
Rom. 2: the righteousness of God
Rom. 3: no one is righteous before God

Rom. 4: since Abraham, righteousness is by faith
Rom. 5: the just are justified by faith in Christ
Rom. 6: the just have died to sin and are made alive to God
Rom. 7: the just have an ongoing struggle with sin
Rom. 8: the just live in the power of the Holy Spirit
Rom. 9–11: the relationship of Israel to the church

Sacrifice is a reasonable response to the mercies of God. But many Christians have difficulty thinking through the implications of a living sacrifice. It is such a foreign concept—a sacrifice is something offered once for all. How do we give ourselves as a "living sacrifice"?

Perhaps the most obvious list of appropriate sacrifices is found in the balance of Romans 12 and 13, a list I have long overlooked. However, if we look at the following verses in a slightly different way, we can see the life lived sacrificially in response to the mercies of God.

### Illustration 10.1
*Living Sacrifices*

| Responses to the Mercies of God | Actual Sacrifice |
|---|---|
| Do not think of yourself more highly than you ought. | pride ego |
| Honor one another above yourselves. | pride |
| We have different gifts . . . use it in proportion to faith. | serving others |
| Hate what is evil; cling to what is good. | your own pet sins |

| Responses to the Mercies of God | Actual Sacrifice |
|---|---|
| Be devoted to one another in brotherly love. | your own agenda |
| Never be lacking in zeal, but keep your spiritual fervor serving the Lord. | comfort convenience |
| Be joyful in hope, patient in affliction | complaining negativism |
| Be . . . faithful in prayer. | pride self-sufficiency |
| Share with God's people who are in need. | material things, money, pride |
| Practice hospitality. | convenience, privacy |
| Bless those who persecute you; bless and do not curse. | rights demand for justice |
| Live in harmony with one another. | individualism private agendas need to control |
| Do not be proud, but be willing to associate with people of low position. | pride, snobbery, status, prejudice |
| Do not be conceited. | selfish desires |
| If it is possible, as far as it depends on you, live at peace with everyone. | need to control |
| Do not take revenge, my friends, but leave room for God's wrath . . . | demand for fairness demand for revenge |

These are living sacrifices! Only one or two are material sacrifices. The rest are related to pride, power, control, and other matters of character and personality. For some people, these are much more daunting sacrifices than a major financial sacrifice.

This sacrificial pattern in response to the mercies of God is consistent with Paul's teaching elsewhere, particularly the Book of Ephesians. In the first three chapters of the six-chapter letter, Paul clearly articulates all the blessings that are ours in Christ:

> Praise be to the God and Father of our Lord Jesus Christ, who has blessed us in the heavenly realms with every spiritual blessing in Christ. For he chose us in him before the creation of the world to be holy and blameless in his sight. In love he predestined us to be adopted as his sons through Jesus Christ in accordance with his pleasure and will—to the praise of his glorious grace, which he has freely given us in the One he loves. [1:3–5]

The second half of the letter, beginning with 4:1, contains Paul's call to us to live a life worthy of who we are in Christ. It is not my purpose to provide a commentary of the fourth, fifth, and sixth chapters of Ephesians. It is important, however, to note how the worthy life to which we are called relates to our worship of God who has called us and qualified us to be holy and blameless in his sight. Four basic areas of sacrifice are called for to live a life worthy of our calling as worshipers of God.

First, Paul calls the worshipers to unity, which requires sacrifice on the part of those with divisive spirits:

> Make every effort to keep the unity of the spirit through the bond of peace. There is one body and one Spirit—just as you were called to one hope when you were called—one Lord, one faith, one baptism; one God and father of all, who is over all and through all and in all. [4:3–5]

Disunity, a mark of immaturity in the body, is an obstacle not only to service, but also to worship. Elsewhere, Paul is quite concerned about the disunity at Corinth. First Corinthians 3 identifies divisions as worldly.

Divisiveness in the church comes from having a variety of agendas among the body rather than a single agenda. Worshipers must strive to maintain the unity of the body if they are to worship. Unity requires the sacrifice of both individual agendas and the desire to control others. That is no small sacrifice in the church.

Second, we must put off the old self as a clearly intentional sacrifice: "You were taught, with regard to your former ways of life, to put off your old self, which is being corrupted by its deceitful desires" (4:22). A quick examination of the specifics given by Paul reveals that many of the elements of the old self are attitudinal and relational: anger, brawling, slander, malice, dishonesty. These qualities bring discord and strife in the body and destroy the unity of the church. We must put off the old self as an act of worship.

Third, Paul calls the church to sacrifice any wrong motives for worship:

> Be very careful, then, how you live—not as unwise but as wise, making the most of every opportunity, because the days are evil. Therefore do not be foolish, but understand what the Lord's will is. Do not get drunk on wine, which leads to debauchery. Instead, be filled with the Spirit. Speak to one another with psalms and hymns and spiritual songs. Sing and make music in your heart to the Lord, always giving thanks to God the Father for everything in the name of our Lord Jesus Christ. [5:15–20]

Sacrifice of wrong motives is essential. How can we suppose to worship God with wrong motives? Because our wrong motives may be very subtle, putting them away may not be easy. Pagan worship might have been openly stimulated by strong drink, but no Christian would agrue for that as helpful for worship.

Just because we are not stimulated by what is obviously wrong does not mean that we are stimulated by what is right! There are other wrong motives, equally as wrong and damaging as alcohol or mood-altering drugs. We can conclude that if we are stimulated by something that is carnal rather than spiritual, then our worship is vain. Worship requires the sacrifice of our carnal motives.

The health-and-wealth gospel offers an example of a stimulus for worship that is corrupted by self-centeredness. As we see the widespread impact of this teaching we can only wonder how many seek God not for himself but for the promise of prosperity.

Akin to the health-and-wealth doctrine is the myth of superspirituality. Superspirituality advances the idea that Spirit-filled worship equates with a mystical experience such as being slain in the Spirit. Those who are motivated by the desire for such an ecstatic experience as the quintessence of worship are really an updated version of those who in the 1970s were intent on getting high on Jesus.

This is not to say that God does not heal or prosper us, or that an encounter with God in worship is primarily a cerebral experience. God does heal. God does prosper us. Meeting God is a deeply emotional experience. However, right worship requires, first of all, our sacrifice of any carnal or self-seeking motives. The greatest sacrifice of true worship may'be the sacrifice of what Stephen Charnock called our demand for satisfaction.

Fourth, Paul calls the body of Christ to the sacrifice of mutual submission: "Submit to one another out of reverence for Christ" (Eph. 5:21). Paul applies this principle broadly —to husbands, wives, slaves, parents, children, and masters. Mutual submission in the body is an act of reverence, an act of worship! Submission requires that we sacrifice our pride, our selfish will, and our desires to control others.

A life worthy of our calling as God's children will require living sacrifice on our parts. So many of these sacrifices are immaterial, yet so often we think of sacrifice in material terms, reflecting our materialistic bias. God has declared his preference for mercy rather than for burnt offerings. Presenting ourselves as living sacrifices is a reasonable act of worship when we understand God's preference.

### *The Model of Sacrificial Worship*

From the opening chapters of Genesis we read that sacrifice is an essential element of acceptable worship. The story of Cain and Abel is a contrast between acceptable and unacceptable offerings to God:

> In the course of time Cain brought some of the fruits of the soil as an offering to the LORD. But Abel brought fat portions from some of the firstborn of his flock. The LORD looked with favor on Abel and his offering, but on Cain and his offering he did not look with favor. [Gen. 4:3–5]

Commentaries abound explaining why Cain's offering was not acceptable. We are told of no prior ordinance from God. We know from later Scriptures that God ordains both animal and grain offerings.

If we borrow from the opening thought of this chapter we can paraphrase the story and perhaps give understanding: Cain offered to God a loaf of bread; Abel, his choicest barbequed ribs. Although God needed neither the grain nor the animal offering, Abel's offering was acceptable because it was sacrificial.

The focus of Genesis quickly turns to Abram, a man who will clearly demonstrate proper worship and acceptable sacrifice. Abram received great reward from God, but Abram never worshiped God for reward.

Abram and his private army of three hundred men set out to rescue Lot and his possessions from the king of Sodom and his allies. Having recovered Lot and his entourage, Abram encountered Melchizedek, the king of Salem (Jerusalem):

> Then Melchizedek king of Salem brought out bread and wine. He was priest of God Most High, and he blessed Abram, saying,
>
> > "Blessed be Abram by God Most High,
> > Creator of heaven and earth.
> > And blessed be God Most High,
> > who delivered your enemies into your hand."
>
> Then Abram gave him a tenth of everything. [14:18–20]
>
> After this, the word of the LORD came to Abram in a vision:
>
> > "Do not be afraid, Abram.
> > I am your shield,
> > your very great reward."
>
> But Abram said, "O Sovereign LORD, what can you give me since I remain childless and the one who will inherit my estate is Eliezer of Damascus?" [15:1–2]

Abram sought no material reward from God because he had everything he needed and had no desire to accumulate more without an heir. The only reward he desired, a son, was far beyond comprehension for a ninety-year-old man and certainly was not his motivation for worship. Yet God blessed Abram with a son, Isaac, at the century mark of his life.

Abraham, as he is now known, was called again by God: "Then God said, 'Take your son, your only son, Isaac, whom you love, and go to the region of Moriah. Sacrifice him there as a burnt offering on one of the mountains I will tell you about'" (22:2). As a father, I cannot comprehend this. Perhaps if God had spoken to me directly six or more times as he had to Abraham, I could have obeyed as Abraham did. I'm not sure.

To Mount Moriah Abraham went with Isaac. We can only wonder what God told Abraham about the mountain or about the time in the future when God would offer his own Son, a descendant of Abraham, on the same mountain. There Abraham obeyed God and offered Isaac to God in his intent and his preparation, if not his execution. Abraham offered Isaac as an intentional act of worship. He told his servants of his intent and his hope: "I and the boy will go over there. We will worship and then we will come back to you" (22:5).

Genesis says that "God tested Abraham." He tests not only Abraham's obedience, but also his motives for worship. Does Abraham worship God because he is the true God or only for the reward? The clearest way to answer that question is to ask Abraham to give back to God the one reward from God that he received and treasured: his son, Isaac. There can be no doubt. Abraham worshiped God for his own sake, and not for a reward. God had spoken clearly: Abraham, I am your reward.

## The Chicken Is Involved, the Pig Is Committed

Abraham models commitment for us. He was fully committed to the worship of God, not simply involved. (We could question whether Isaac was committed or just involved!) How different is Abraham's attitude toward worship than ours. Although Abraham must have come off the mountain exultant, he did not go up the mountain in search of a religious experience. He went in obedience to God's directive: Come and worship me!

Abraham worshiped God because he was committed to God's glory and not to his own needs, his own feelings, or his own agenda. Abraham, a committed worshiper (figuratively, a pig) differs radically from the involved (chicken) worshipers in the church today.

In our era of human-centered Christianity, many people honestly consider themselves committed. In reality, they are committed to themselves. They are committed to having their needs met. They are committed to their own spiritual satisfaction in worship rather than God's. They are committed to having mountaintop experiences, but without taking a sacrifice with them. They feel committed! It's not the same kind of commitment that Abraham demonstrated.

Worship today often lacks sacrifice. Without some element of sacrifice, worship easily becomes focused on ourselves, on our needs and on our satisfaction. True worship has a high cost.

## The Sacrifice Needed to Revive Our Worship

To say that we need revival may conjure up confusing images. But we need to revive our worship. Revival is not church growth, although revival often brings church growth. In fact, it is easy to conclude that our worship is acceptable because our church is growing. It is not always true! Church growth principles have, in part, led some astray into consumer-oriented churches that have nurtured commitment to self and satisfaction more than a commitment to glorify God.

How will revival come to our worship and to our churches? That is our vital concern as we conclude.

# RENEWING OUR WORSHIP

A number of worship themes need to
be thought through by evangelicals as we
reform our worship. We need to recognize
and come to terms with the reflective
nature of our style of worship. Perhaps
even we stiff, white evangelicals can learn
from our black, Jewish and charismatic
brethren. At the same time we need to
open ourselves to instruction from our
liturgical brothers and sisters.
Dr. David Fisher,
Park Street Church, Boston,
*United Evangelical Action*

## The Call for Revival

It was a serendipity. Sorting through some old files, I found
a tattered copy of an early article from the *Wittenburg Door*.
It caught my attention at once:

A better clue to what has gone wrong with worship can be
found, ironically, in the volume of materials that have come

forth in the last decade to revitalize worship. In the vast
majority of these, the effort has been directed toward making worship more contemporary and spontaneous, and more
focused on the experience of the worshiper.

   . . . [the worship renewal movement] has missed this fundamental truth, too often referring to what happens on Sunday morning as a "worship experience." The experience
referred to is not how Christ has experienced our praise and
worship, but how we, the so-called worshipers have.

   Again, much of worship renewal has bowed to the spirit
of the age and allowed itself to get trapped into a consumer
approach to worship. The narcissism of our time has left its
stamp on the church and many Christians come to worship
drastically out of focus. There to "get religion" rather than
give adoration.

   Solidly Christian worship will never come from people who
have the expectations of a consumer oriented, narcissistic,
amorphously spontaneous "now generation."[1]

I've had a growing sense for some time that something is
not right with what we in the church call worship. It is at
least reassuring to know that I was not alone in my perception. The *Door* is on target—much of the contemporary worship renewal in the church has led only to more self-
centered Christianity.

   In 1988 I moved to Southern California, the promised
land of the megachurch and the home of the church growth
movement. Five years in Southern California not only
opened my eyes, but also intensified my sense of uneasiness
with various blips I have picked up on my radar as I have
scanned the evangelical countryside. Perhaps most disturb-
ing was a comment made to me by a district superintendent
of a major evangelical denomination. He told me that successful ministry, at least in Southern California, is based on
image and appearance rather than on substance. The radar

images have begun to form a pattern that I can begin to describe.

First, I've become uneasy watching my generation and my parents' generation in combat over musical tastes (worship songs versus old gospel songs). Both the traditionalists and the proponents of contemporary worship seem equally selfish in their concern about how satisfying worship is to them. Each has a different set of criteria, but both share a concern for how they enjoy worship. There is a great need for today's worshipers to learn to sacrifice for even an hour a week their demand that every piece of music meet with their approval. Only a renewed understanding of worship can bring that.

Second, although we need revival, I've been uneasy with what many seem to perceive as the meaning of revival and with the methods some would employ to bring revival. Revival is the sovereign work of a sovereign Holy Spirit who is not to be manipulated by those who think they have cornered the market. Moreover, revival is not church growth. Revival will often bring church growth, but it is not the same thing. It is easy to conclude that revival has come and that our worship is acceptable because our church is growing. It is not always true!

Church growth principles have led some to nurture a consumer-oriented church where commitment to self and self-satisfaction from God supersede a commitment to glorify God.

Revival, the supernatural work of the Spirit of God restoring his people to holiness through an new encounter with the holy God, is needed. Revival begins with prayer, seeking God for himself. It leads to repentance, forsaking the self-centeredness of the age that we have embraced. It leads to healing in the church, restoring unity and singleness of purpose. It leads to service, motivated properly by the Holy Spirit. It leads to commitment, leaving the merely involved behind. It leads to worship in Spirit and in truth, where sacrifice is willingly given. But revival is not an "orgy of emotions," as some might lead us to believe.[2]

Third, while we have sharpened our marketing skills, it appears that we are not making an impact on our American culture. Southern California, for example, with all its megachurches and radio and television ministries, is leading the national decline in church participation, now under 40 percent. When the church succeeds more at consolidating Christian people in a limited number of larger churches than in reaching non-Christians, what have we accomplished for the kingdom of God? New associations of megachurches that cross traditional denominational lines are springing up. And, we might well ask, to what ultimate end?

The perceived importance of what is happening in California makes this trend critical. Auto manufacturers, led by the Japanese, have located their design centers in California on the theory that if they can successfully design, build, and sell cars to the thirty million West-Coast residents, they will be successful nationally with that product and on their way to global success.

One must be concerned with the perceived importance of the church in California. So many ministries are in California (even in light of the exodus to Colorado Springs) that the North American church seems uncritically influenced by the disproportionate number of high-profile ministries on the West Coast.

We do not appear to be keeping the critical balance between the goal of God-centered worship and gospel of God's love for fallen humanity. I've invested the first ten chapters building my case for God-centered worship and the need to swim against the tide of human-centeredness that is flooding the church. There are no easy formulas for reviving our worship. But we can begin by asking God to revive our worship as we open our eyes wide and focus on what worship should be according to God's design.

## Who's Squeezing the Church?

It should come as little surprise that immediately after Paul challenged the church in Rome to offer themselves as living sacrifices—as an act of spiritual worship (Rom. 12:1)—he warned them not to allow the world to squeeze them into its mold (12:2).

The world has established many patterns that the church uses. We can review much of where we have been if we look at present trends in terms of how the church has been conforming to the pattern of this world. The values of the world have been spilling over into the church at an alarming rate in this generation. While there are many portals where the influence is spilling in, I am primarily concerned with three because of the impact each has upon worship.

First, and perhaps most significantly, we have conformed to the basic mold of success. We have emulated our society by making success the yardstick for ministry and the church. Evangelical Rodney Clapp, writing in the *Wall Street Journal*, argues that evangelicals "are clearly infatuated with outward signs of success," calling this an age that judges everything by "quantifications and statistics."[3]

Our preoccupation with nickels and noses reflects the success orientation of the culture. The church must seek to reach every lost person, but we must recover the awareness that Jesus attempted to give his disciples: "For wide is the gate and broad is the way that leads to destruction, and many enter through it. But small is the gate and narrow the road that leads to life, and only a few find it" (Matt. 7:13–14). Immediately after Jesus taught this, he turned his attention in the Sermon on the Mount to false prophets. He warns against the false prophets because they will mislead people into thinking they belong to Christ when, in fact, they do not. He utters the chilling warning:

"Not everyone who says to me, 'Lord, Lord,' will enter the kingdom of heaven, but only he who does the will of my Father who is in heaven. Many will say to me on that day, 'Lord, Lord, did we not prophecy in your name, and in your name drive out demons and perform many miracles?' Then I will tell them plainly, 'I never knew you. Away from me, you evil doers!'" [7:21–23]

The most dangerous place to which a false prophet can lead people is not away from God but toward him! The false prophet leads people to a place of false security in the shadow of the church, where they mistakenly think they are part of the kingdom. The danger is greatest because these who are so led astray are unaware of their condition and never have reason to question it. They may see miracles and hear prophecies in Jesus' name, never suspecting that they are on the outside looking in.

There is a far more subtle danger of buying into the success orientation than the obvious false prophets or celebrity cults masquerading as churches. The desire to succeed in ministry is seductive, especially when it can be rationalized in the name of the kingdom of God.

We may actually perform an ultimate and eternal disservice by misleading people into an "easy believeism," thinking they are true believers when they are not. A strong success orientation breeds the temptation to make the gospel more inclusive than it really is by making it something other than what it really is. The temptation grows to enormous proportions in an age when rampant existentialism and narcissism have created a conducive environment for such error. The needed corrective must come from the biblical truth. God calls the church to faithfulness, not success.

Hudson Taylor Amerding, former president of Wheaton College, initiated his thoughtful discussion of leadership by reminding us, "Anyone called of God to Christian leadership should recognize that he or she will be working with a minority in our society. Awareness of the meaning of our minority status is essential to effective leadership."[4] God calls us to be faithful leaders, not successful leaders. When faithfulness, the paradigm of Scripture, has been replaced by success, then we must take heed. The church that is preoccupied by success is being squeezed into the world's mold.

Second, the church seems to be increasingly conformed to the world's ideas about service rather than God's. It is not news that our economy is shifting rapidly from a manufacturing base to a service base. The shift is founded on a growing demand in our society for service. Since it is often easier to transport products than services, we are buying, as a nation, more foreign-made products and diverting increased quantities of our resources to providing services. As Americans have a diminishing amount of discretionary time available each week,[5] they are consuming services, such as eating more meals in restaurants and buying more domestic services.

The church is being squeezed into the same mold. That is not to say that Christians should not hire gardeners to cut the grass, or eat in restaurants, or that they must change their own motor oil. But we must be aware of how the service orientation has affected the church: it is moving us toward accepting the church as a business that markets (successfully or unsuccessfully) religious services. This view replaces the understanding of the church as the body of Christ of which we are each parts.

The *Wall Street Journal* confirmed this trend, suggesting that the measurable pattern of giving to the church by baby boomers reflects the growing consumerism in the church: "Some researchers and educators also cite a rising 'consumerist' mentality in U.S. Churches. . . . People have changed from stewards into consumers . . . where they are buying specific services—youth program, a music program."[6] Again, as we noted in chapter 4, even the secular media are

surprised how far the church is willing to go to attract baby
boomers who will engage the church only on their terms. In
other words, even those outside the church can see how much
the church is willing to let the world shape it.

How radically different from the Word of God is the shape
to which the world seems to be squeezing the church. Jesus,
after all, said:

> "You know that the rulers of the Gentiles lord it over them.
> . . . Not so with you. Instead, whoever wants to become great
> among you must be your servant, and whoever wants to be
> first must be your slave—just as the Son of Man did not come
> to be served, but to serve . . ." [Matt. 20:25–28]

The New Testament calls the disciples of Jesus Christ to be
servants. As we have noted, the challenge facing the church
is how to transform consumers of church services into
servants. It seems that the church is willing to let professing
Christians remain consumers indefinitely. We send mixed
messages when we blindly apply marketing principles to the
church and fail to see that we are at the same time marketing
to the unchurched and promoting Christian consumerism.

We must move professing believers beyond their immaturity as merely consumers of religious services who will forever be shopping for the best value without feeling any sense
of loyalty or obligation.

The revitalization of worship is necessary if we are ever
to enable immature and narcissistic Christians to move out
from among the ranks of the "served" to become servants.
We must model in our worship the pattern of Isaiah, who
saw the Lord, was purged of sin, and volunteered for service. We must take the focus off ourselves and our needs
and move it onto God through a basic tenet of our faith: "For
Christ's love compels us, because we are convinced that one
died for all, and therefore all died. And he died for all, that
*those who live should no longer live for themselves but for him*

*who died for them* and was raised again" (2 Cor. 5:14–15, italics added). It is in genuine worship that the power of God transforms us from people who live for themselves to people who live for him who died for us.

Third, as we noted in chapter 5, existentialism has encroached on the twentieth-century church like a malignant tumor. James Engel acknowledges that the "existential heresy" is clearly evident in the "excess of the health and wealth gospel." It is a subjective truth that oils the machinery of existentialism. It has seduced the church into focusing on felt needs and desires rather than on real needs.[7] Existentialism has lured the church into thinking that how we feel (desires) and what we experience (the fulfillment of those desires) are the guides to truth. Existentialism has diverted the church from its focus on kingdom values to a focus on earthly values.[8]

This view diverges radically from our historic Christian faith because it runs counter to the unchanging nature of the Word of God. Moreover, it runs up against the Christian world view that the unseen reality of the spiritual world is the higher reality: "So we fix our eyes not on what is seen, but on what is unseen. For what is seen is temporary, but what is unseen is eternal" (2 Cor. 4:18). Again, it is in worship that we take our eyes off the temporal and fix them on the eternal. We can understand if our evangelism appears human-centered in our efforts to find common ground. But if our worship is focused on human needs, problems, and issues for the sake of being practical and relevant, how will this transformation in our lives ever take place? How will we ever embrace a thoroughly Christian world view if we insist that everything in the ministry of the church fit a materialistic matrix?

These three areas—our success orientation, our service orientation, and our embrace of existentialism—are only some of the ways the church has bowed to the culture. The world has been squeezing the church into its mold and our human-centered Christianity and human-centered worship is merely the composite result.

## Renewing Our Minds

Immediately after Paul exhorted Christians to not conform to the pattern of the world, he wrote a prescription for those afflicted with the various cancers of the age: "be transformed by the renewing of your minds." There are a number of ways to fill that prescription.

*Restoring personal worship is essential to renewing corporate worship.* Much of the confusion and division we have over worship is the result of a truncated understanding of worship as a group experience that takes place 1 or 2 hours out of a 168-hour week. If that is what the church understands worship to be, then that hour becomes loaded with unrealistic expectations that can only lead to disappointment.

Every pastor has had to confront the expectations of one or more church members who want to receive a weekly transfusion of grace, faith, hope, encouragement, inspiration, and blessing from a one-hour service with a thirty-minute message. They come seeking to get their batteries charged (or to get spiritually pumped up) in order to make it through the week. They barely make it, it often seems.

Every week we need to hear from God, and certainly there are weeks when that need is critical. Of course there are times when we pant for God as we enter into corporate worship. But, if the spiritual condition of a large group of Christians is regularly likened to a battery that continually discharges or a tire with a slow leak, what does that say about their true spiritual condition? If God's people come together collectively needing to be spiritually jump-started each Sunday, there is clearly something wrong.

Both the continual migration in search of a better church and the ubiquitous conflict in churches trying to find a style of worship pleasing to old and young alike are rooted in the same unfulfilled expectations. The disappointment that some feel with worship is a result of the unrealistic expectations they project onto a corporate worship experience. No one would expect to be either satisfied or well nourished in one feeding a week, regardless of the quantity and quality of the meal. Yet many expect that in one weekly corporate worship experience all their needed spiritual transactions should take place.

The same can be said for those who come to the corporate gathering of the church with unrealistic expectations concerning evangelism. To expect that the church's evangelistic purpose can be accomplished in 2/168ths of the week will disappoint as well.

What is missing is private worship. Corporate worship can never adequately stand alone in the life of the believer. Regular personal worship is essential for a number of reasons. First, in private worship we learn to enter into God's presence. Second, we learn that worship is not and cannot be a performance put on by others. We cultivate an appreciation for worship leaders as the prompters or the sponsors of worship. Third, we learn how to follow the leading of the Holy Spirit as he leads us in worship, to clearly distinguish his voice. Fourth, we learn in private how demanding worship can be. Worship can be hard work, and private worship certainly explodes any contrary myths. Fifth, because we are free in private worship to express ourselves in the way that we most value or in a way we feel most conducive to worship, we are free to worship corporately. In private worship I can discharge my private agenda for worship and be released to worship with a group with no agenda or selfish demands of my own.

Cultivating private worship radically changes corporate worship because it prepares us for corporate worship. It is not unlike the lesson I learned when a friend in the Vienna Symphony invited me to a rehearsal. Each musician in each section prepares from his own score. He rehearses each selection repeatedly in the privacy of his own office or rehearsal room. The goal is to be proficient with each piece so that each musician can focus his eyes on the conductor. Hours of private rehearsal are needed to play the various sections of the score, as well as scales to keep the skills sharp. All this must be invested individually before the orchestra tackles a new piece of music together. As the orchestra gathers for rehearsal in the afternoon, various different musical voices blend in harmony to create a single sound. No one plays every note, for different instruments solo and come in and out as the score requires. Each musician, however, pays careful attention to follow every measure on his own page as others play. Each is prepared to come in as cued by the conductor's gesture. The conductor himself plays no instrument but leads the various string and woodwind and brass and percussion instruments in a single interpretation and expression. The orchestra, because it knows the opus thoroughly, is able to follow the lead of the conductor and play the same piece a number of different expressive ways.

How different our worship together would be if the church understood this concept, a concept rooted deeply in the Old Testament prescription for the choirs and orchestra at the dedication of the temple. How different our corporate worship would be if each believer prepared in private and small-group worship each week for that climactic moment when God's people come together to offer to God our corporate worship! Even the contemporary emphasis on being spontaneous and responsive to the Holy Spirit's leading can only be enhanced by being thoroughly prepared for worship. Those of a more traditional and liturgical style must cope with being well prepared in order to keep from becoming stale.

*The dramatic nature of worship must be rediscovered if worship is to be revived.* The worship dramas of the Bible instruct us. Moses at the burning bush is a vignette of worship. Isaiah's vision of heavenly worship is part of a one-act drama. In the fourth and fifth chapters of Revelation we see the grandest drama of worship in the Bible.

In Act 1, the set is described: the throne in heaven surrounded by a sea of crystal. The four living creatures enter in their striking and symbolic attire. They announce the program as they declare the holiness of the triune God. The elders join in worship, laying their crowns before the throne and ascribing the worthiness of God to receive worship from every creature present.

Act 2 opens with a mystery. Who can open the scroll? Who can break the seal to the final act? Despair sweeps through the cast as no one worthy is found. Then, the great hero of the drama, the Lamb, enters. He will open the scroll.

Act 2 ends with two new songs sung as the drama reaches a climactic moment. The chorus sings to the Lamb "You Are Worthy." They are joined by an unnumbered choir who sing "Worthy Is the Lamb." Finally, everyone in the audience joins in the great song of praise to the Lamb. It is great drama, a drama that leads to the culmination of all human history. In the following chapters the armies of God march out to conquest with the trumpet blast announcing that the kindgom of this world has become the kingdom of our God and of his Christ! The final act brings a great banquet in heaven when the people of God will feast on the rulers of the world. It is a drama which we need to revive and of which we cannot grow tired.

We need to think of this drama as we do of a videotape of a favorite musical production. My daughter will watch repeatedly the Disney animation of *Cinderella*. She not only knows every line of dialogue and the words of every song but also speaks and sings along freely. Her familiarity has not made the story any less wonderful. Rather, it is more wonderful, for she savors her recitation. She knows the outcome, of course, but enjoys the wedding of Cinderella and the prince as much the hundredth time as she did the first. The drama never grows old.

Many have returned to liturgical expressions of worship in order to find more dramatic idioms of worship.[9] The mass, for all its unacceptable theology of transubstantiation, does present and preserve a dramatic approach to worship. For those committed to contemporary expressions of worship, it may not be necessary to return to the Book of Common Prayer or the lectionary to revive the sense of drama in worship. Creative use of music and Scripture readings moving toward high moments of praise can provide the same sense of drama.

I need only to recall one worship experience to remind me of the importance and relative simplicity of reviving drama. There were only a handful of us in a doctoral class at Bethel Seminary. We concluded the class on the Psalms with a worship service for which the planning spanned the whole week. The sense of drama was established when we began with a processional as the tiny band moved to the chapel singing and reading the Songs of Ascent (Pss. 120–134).

Drama (to return to an earlier concept in this discussion) involves a sense of movement—sometimes the movement of people, other times the movement of events toward a designated outcome. In the age of passive television-trained worshipers, it is the drama of worship that will involve people. Drama involves worshipers in the action in the same way that old radio soap operas involved listeners. Using drama in worship has its place, but we must keep in mind the goal of making the whole of worship a drama.

*The purpose and mission of the church must be renewed and cultivated.* We cannot assume, as we may have in previous generations, that lay leaders or the members of the church clearly understand or fully endorse the purpose of the church. We have good reason to believe that evangelicals today are less theologically discerning than their grandparents. Even if the right words are used—worship, evangelize, kingdom of God, global missions—there is reason to suspect that many evangelicals today either don't understand or don't fully embrace the purpose of the church as they have in the past.[10]

We must urgently renew our sense of purpose. Every church needs to write or rewrite its mission statement and develop broad ownership of that statement. This is needed to restore what has eroded our collective grasp of the mission of the church. In fact, the trend toward clearly written mission statements for organizations is an encouraging and fairly recent phenomenon. In previous generations there appears to have been an assumption that the Great Commission was an adequate declaration of purpose.

Few have articulated the importance and role of a purpose statement for the church as well as Rick Warren at Saddleback Community Church in Mission Viejo, California. The church has a manageable mission statement, one that is carefully applied to everything the church does. A major step in writing a mission statement, argues Warren, is for a church to ask four questions based on essential biblical study of important New Testament passages:

Who are we?
What are we?
Why do we exist?
What does God expect us to do?[11]

That the church needs to ask these questions implies that many church members do not have clear answers to these questions. Renewing our worship requires that we renew our understanding of our purpose.

For a church seeking a mission statement related to the centrality of worship, I would offer the following example as a starting point:

*The purpose of*

_____

*shall be to glorify God*
*by*
*engaging his creation and our community*
*with the gospel of Jesus Christ*
*in order to*
*recruit,*
*disciple,*
*equip,*
*release, and*
*empower worshipers*
*who, as living sacrifices,*
*are collectively seeking*
*to evangelize the*
*whole world.*

*Renewing a worship character is a final area of renewal that appears to be urgently needed.* The God who qualified us to worship has prescribed for us the character of worshipers that is pleasing to him. These are sprinkled in many places in Scripture, but a little exploring in Psalms 95 to 100 will reveal seven qualities we must cultivate if we are to revive worship and restore God-centered worship to the church.

**Humility.** Only the humble can worship because the true worshiper is aware that he stands before God empty-handed—without merit of his own, only by grace. We may come boldly, but only if we understand that it is truly a throne of grace to which we come.

How far afield is the feel-good theology of self-esteem that argues that "once a person believes he is an unworthy sinner, it is doubtful if he can really honestly accept the saving grace God offers in Jesus Christ."[12] The Psalms tell us otherwise:

> In his hand are the depths of the earth,
> 　　and the mountain peaks belong to him.
> The sea is his, for he made it,
> 　　his hands formed the dry land.
>
> Come, let us bow down in worship,
> 　　let us kneel before the LORD our Maker;
> for he is our God
> 　　and we are the people of his pasture,
> 　　the flock under his care. [Ps. 95:4–7]
>
> It is he who made us, and we are his;
> 　　we are his people, the sheep of his pasture. [Ps. 100:3]

**Open, teachable spirits.** Humble people are open and eager to learn every time they hear God's Word. It is the proud who are content with their spiritual attainment, and this contentment fosters pride in one's spiritual attainment. The psalmist encourages the teachable character:

> Today, if you hear his voice,
> 　　do not harden your hearts as you did at Meribah,
> 　　as you did that day at Massah in the desert,
> where your fathers tested and tried me,
> 　　though they had seen what I did.
> For forty years I was angry with that generation;
> 　　I said, "They are a people whose hearts go astray,
> 　　and they have not known my ways."
> So I declared on oath in my anger,
> 　　"They shall never enter my rest." [Ps. 95:8–11]

It is worth noting how often the Psalms speak of singing new songs. New songs are for open and teachable people. We can only speculate what archtraditionalists will do when someone tries to teach them new songs in heaven.

**Joy.** The second fruit of the Holy Spirit, joy is an inner quality of wellness that comes not from material circumstances but from higher spiritual realities. There can be no higher joy than to be in communion with the God who created us to worship and enjoy him.

How different is joy from happiness. Happiness depends upon what is happening about us. We must keep the distinction in mind because so much of what we call worship seeks to make believers happy but does not produce joy. When believers think that true worship equates with happiness, or its kin, ecstasy, they have fallen into the trap of our age, in which happiness is touted as a counterfeit for joy.

God wants joyful worshipers:

> Come, let us sing for joy to the LORD;
>   let us shout aloud to the Rock of our salvation.
> Let us come before him with thanksgiving
>   and extol him with music and song.
>
> For the LORD is the great God,
>   the great King above all gods. [Ps. 95:1–3]
>
> Shout for joy to the LORD, all the earth,
>   burst into jubilant song with music;
> make music to the LORD with the harp,
>   with the harp and the sound of singing,
> with trumpets and the blast of the ram's horn—
>   shout for joy before the LORD, the King. [Ps. 98:4–6]
>
> Shout for joy to the LORD, all the earth.
>   Worship the LORD with gladness;
>   come before him with joyful songs. [Ps. 100:1–2]

**Reverence.** If we are to revive worship, we must cultivate anew a reverence for the holy and sovereign God. Loss of the sense of the holy has eroded our reverence. The demanding name-it-and-claim-it theology that seemingly treats God as a cosmic genie who needs only to be rubbed the right way has even further eroded our reverence. Martin Marty suggests that many evangelicals treat "God like a big contact in their Rolodex file."[13] If we cannot find deep reverence being cultivated among evangelicals on their way into the sanctuary—often late for their appointment with God—where will we find it? It can come from the worship manual of the people who knew firsthand that mortals died when they entered in the presence of God irreverently:

> For great is the LORD and most worthy of praise;
>    he is to be feared above all gods.
> For all the gods of the nations are idols,
>    but the LORD made the heavens.
> Splendor and majesty are before him;
>    strength and glory are in his sanctuary.
>
> Ascribe to the LORD, O families of nations,
>    ascribe to the LORD glory and strength.
> Ascribe to the LORD the glory due his name;
>    bring an offering and come into his courts.
> Worship the LORD in the splendor of his holiness;
>    tremble before him, all the earth. [Ps. 96:4–9]

British theologian J. S. Whale has captured the contemporary attitude: "Instead of putting off our shoes from our feet because the place we stand is holy ground, we are taking nice photographs of the burning bush from suitable angles."[14]

I cannot help but appreciate David McKenna's analysis of reverence as he expressed his longing for its return. "The truth is," he wrote, "our worship can be polluted by our care-lessness, our selfishness, and a secularism." Carelessness shows in our corporate preparation, lack of punctuality, and lack of personal preparation. Selfishness is synonymous with human-centeredness: Centered on ourselves and our needs, "we miss God" in our anticipation of a "psychological bath of emotion, entertainment, or enthusiasm." Secularism and its material world view sap the wonder out of worship.[15] Together these three infestations eat away our sense of awe and wonder in worship.

The Spruce Goose, Howard Hughes's enormous flying boat, was recently dismantled and moved from its museum home in Long Beach to the Pacific Northwest. Stories of the project reminded me of the first time I peeked at the world's largest airplane. The Goose sat under a black dome. Its white hulk was illuminated from below by brilliant white lights. The sight of this massive airship was sudden as I entered the exhibit hall, and I stopped in my tracks, overwhelmed by this white-on-black silhouette. It's only a wooden air-plane, but I remember the impact was awesome as I felt dwarfed, even puny, near a plane nearly twice the size of the DC-10 I had just been on. As people entered the hall, they lowered their voices; some took off their hats, as they might when entering a cathedral. If God's people entered into the sactuary of the church with as much awe, there would be a marked changed as soon as this Sunday.

**World perspective.** We sense this in this most instruc-tive group of Psalms. A global perspective would be a nat-ural outcome of worshipers who draw near to God seeking to have his heart. Evangelism grows out of worship as we also worship Christ for the same reason as the host in heaven: "you purchased men for God from every tribe and language and people and nation."

> Declare his glory among the nations,
>     his marvelous deeds among all peoples.

For great is the LORD and most worthy of praise;
  he is to be feared above all gods.
For all the gods of the nations are idols,
  but the LORD made the heavens.
Splendor and majesty are before him;
  strength and glory are in his sanctuary.

Ascribe to the LORD, O families of nations,
  ascribe to the LORD glory and strength.
Ascribe to the LORD the glory due his name;
  bring an offering and come into his courts.
Worship the LORD in the splendor of his holiness;
  tremble before him, all the earth.

Say among the nations, "The LORD reigns."
  The world is firmly established, it cannot be moved;
  he will judge the peoples with equity. [Ps. 96:3–10]

The LORD reigns,
    let the nations tremble;
  he sits enthroned between the cherubim,
    let the earth shake.
  Great is the LORD in Zion; . . .
    he is holy. [Ps. 99:1–3]

One of the struggles I have long had with church growth
principles is the principle of homogeneity, which gives tacit
validation to ethnic segregation. This flies in the face of God's
plan for a church drawn from all of fifteen thousand people
groups. It may be a sociological truth that people prefer to
worship and fellowship with people ethnically and socio-
economically like themselves. Demographics have never been
a good test of what is right and wrong, however. Hetero-
geneity, not homogeneity, is the heavenly model for the worshiping church in heaven and the practical model for the
functioning church on earth. We may plant Chinese churches

and Hispanic congregations, but we should have a goal of integrating our ethnic congregations as an offering to God.

Those who have had the privilege of worshiping in international assemblies with fifty to a hundred nations represented know the remarkable joy of this foretaste of heavenly worship. Because it not only inspires our worship, but also ignites our evangelism, we must whenever we can cultivate worship that embraces the whole world.

**Aversion to evil.** Sin always poisons worship. Of course, in nearly any church all manner of hidden sins lurk beneath the surface. But, one could argue that what is more destructive to worship than a closet alcoholic or an adulterous elder is the pharisaism that we encounter in some evangelical circles.

Pharisaism poisons worship because it promotes legalism rather than zeal for true righteousness. Jesus said that the result of pharisaism is persons who worship God outwardly while their hearts are far away. The Pharisees and their modern counterparts miss the hunger and thirst for true righteousness with their microscopic focus on those laws they keep carefully. Today's pharisees have developed a clever trick to avoid dealing with real evil, or what Jesus called the weightier matters of the law. They shoot the arrow first, then draw the target around it. They say they have hit the target of righteousness every time, but all they have done is redefine righteousness in terms of the specific sins they don't commit. How many churches, for example, have written into their creeds, covenants, or constitutions prohibitions against any use of alcohol but fail to mention the real sins that are far more destructive to the church: gossip, slander, envy, bitterness, and resentment?

The Word of God calls for a zeal for real righteousness that hates real evil.

> Let those who love the LORD hate evil,
>    for he guards the lives of his faithful ones
>    and delivers them from the hand of the wicked.

> Light is shed upon the righteous
> and joy on the upright in heart.
> Rejoice in the LORD, you who are righteous,
> and praise his holy name. [Ps. 97:10–12]

Being in fellowship with a holy God changes how we think and feel about sin in our own lives.

Being in communion with a righteous but gracious God also changes how we think and feel about sin in the lives of others. Chuck Swindoll unvarnishes the truth for us: "We can become the most severe, condemning, judgmental, guilt-giving people on the face of planet earth, and we claim it's in the name of Jesus Christ. And all the while, we don't even know we're doing it. That's the pathetic part of it all."[16] Jesus pointed to the Pharisee who thanked God he was not like other men. This unnamed Pharisee was unable to worship because his misguided zeal led to proud legalism. We must cultivate a zeal for true righteousness that can alone extinguish the rampant pharisaism of our day.

**Appreciation for the privilege of worship.** Again and again in this section of Psalms we are told how all of God's creation worships him: the rocks, the heavens, the trees, the rivers. I don't think we can dismiss this as mere poetry. Nor can it be dismissed as incidental when it is mentioned in three consecutive psalms.

> Say among the nations, "The LORD reigns."
> The world is firmly established, it cannot be moved;
> he will judge the peoples with equity.
> Let the heavens rejoice, let the earth be glad;
> let the sea resound, and all that is in it;
> let the fields be jubilant, and everything in them.
> Then all the trees of the forest will sing for joy;
> they will sing before the LORD, for he comes,
> he comes to judge the earth. [Ps. 96:10–13]

The LORD reigns, let the earth be glad;
   let the distant shores rejoice.

The heavens proclaim his righteousness,
   and all the peoples see his glory. [Ps. 97:1, 6]

Let the sea resound, and everything in it,
   the world, and all who live in it.
Let the rivers clap their hands,
   let the mountains sing together for joy;
let them sing before the LORD, . . . [Ps. 98:7–9]

What are we to make of all this? The truth is that God does not need our worship. He receives continual worship from a countless host of heavenly beings. The Psalms inform us that he even receives praise from what we classify as inanimate objects—rivers, mountains, and seas. Keeping in mind that "God can make sons of Abraham out of the rocks," we are in awe of what God has done.

He has ordained praise from a sinful, self-willed, rebellious, stiff-necked race of people whom he created a little lower than the angels. Because he loves us, he has called us and at infinite cost qualified us to "join with all nature in manifold witness!" We have been invited to join in worship with the trees, the rivers, and the earth itself.

## A Final Thought

I began to study worship because I had a hunger for worship of God that transports God's people from the outer courts into the Holy of Holies—into the presence of God. I was motivated in part by a comment from Chuck Colson: that he didn't want to learn how to get more out of his Christian life, but wanted to learn how to put more in.

The veil in the Holy Place has been torn down by the death of Christ, yet so many remain outside and never come in.

There on the perimeter of the Holy Place we find all sorts of people. There are those in the elaborate booths selling self-help programs. Around the corner, others sell maps and pictures of what the temple is like inside. Why bother to enter? Just buy the tour book with all the color pictures. For a few dollars more, videotapes can be ordered. Wandering around are scalpers selling tickets to the grandstands inside where many go only to watch others worship. Rumors now abound that luxury boxes are planned for the select few who can afford them. Everywhere, it seems, there are security people who make sure only the right kinds of people are allowed inside.

How far we have come from Sam Shoemaker, who wrote a generation ago that he "stood by the door" to direct others inside. Standing by the door required not staying inside the door all the time and not wandering too far away. It is the most important door in the world, the door by which people may enter to find God.

I have written this for all those who share my concern for the church of Jesus Christ. I'm concerned with the trends I have articulated in these pages. I have more questions than answers, but perhaps the questions themselves will help the church to refocus on its task. I think these are days when we have no time to play church or to get bogged down in selfish intramural debates. Over my desk hangs a plaque:

> *The main thing*
> *is to keep*
> *the main thing*
> *the main thing!*

Worshiping the right God in the right way is the main thing.

# ENDNOTES

## Introduction: Do You Know His Name?

1. *Mongolian Enterprise Newsletter*, Fall 1991.

2. A noted Christian scientist, Hugh Ross, seeking to integrate the biblical account of creation with scientific data, cites the appearance on the anthropological stage of a distinct new species. Concurrent with the appearance of this new species is the appearance of evidence of worship and religion. See "The Search for Adam and Eve," *Newsweek*, 11 January 1988.

Thomas Maugh II writes that the recent reclassifications of Neanderthals into the human family tree has caused many scientists to rethink the "African Eve Theory." The debate could seemingly continue without in any way changing Ross's approach. See "Study Boosts Neanderthal," *Los Angeles Times*, 9 February 1992, A–1, A–12.

3. Quoted in Richard Higgins, "Americans' Interest in Religion Is Shallow," *The Orange County Register*, 22 April 1991, A–8.

## Chapter 1: Worship in the Church Growth Era

1. James Berkley, "Church Growth Comes of Age," *Leadership* (Fall 1991): 108.

2. John MacArthur and the editors of *Leadership*, "Our Sufficiency for Outreach," Leadership (Fall 1991): 138.

3. Kathleen Newmeyer, "God for Sale," *Los Angeles Magazine*, February 1989, 170–71.

4. Robert H. Schuller, in *Self-Esteem, the New Reformation* (Waco: Word, 1982), clearly sought to write a new orthodoxy and to abandon the Reformation. His statement that "sin is thinking that you are not worthy of God's grace" embraces enough unbiblical theology to have risked burning at the stake in earlier eras of the church. Chapter 4 will deal with this more fully.

5. *National and International Religion* Report, 7, 20 (20 September, 1993).

6. Carl Horton, "Church Dynamics," lecture given at the Kellogg Center, Pomona, California, May 1991.

7. Jack Simms, lecture given at the National Small Group Workers Conference, Fuller Theological Seminary, Pasadena, California, 1989.

8. Kenneth S. Kantzer and Carl F. H. Henry, *Evangelical Roots* (Deerfield, Ill.: Trinity Evangelical Divinity School and InterVarsity, 1992) videotape lectures, part 4.

# Chapter 2: Worshiping the Right God

1. Quoted in *Our Daily Bread*, 21 April 1992.

2. Stephen Charnock, *The Existence and Attributes of God*.

3. The common ontological, teleological, and cosmological arguments for the existence of God are all valuable to a point, and all are based upon the principles of Romans 1:18–22. The moral argument, made popular by C. S. Lewis in *Mere Christianity* (New York: Macmillan, 1952), is based on a different foundation, the innate sense of right and wrong in the human heart.

4. The name of God revealed to Moses in Exodus 3:14–15 is YHWH in Hebrew, transliterated Yahweh in English. Many Bible readers are not aware that, wherever YHWH appears in the original text, English translators have substituted LORD. YHWH is made up of two parts. *Y* is the third person masculine prefix, and *HWH* is the root of the verb to be. He is also known by other names, such as Elohim (God) and El Shaddai (God almighty). Exodus 6:7 instructs us that YHWH is the covenantal name by which God would be known by his people.

5. Don Richardson, *Eternity in Their Hearts*, rev. ed. (Ventura, Calif.: Regal, 1981).

6. Alistair Begg, "Acceptable Worship" (Paramount, Calif.: Grace to You Tape Ministry, 1991), audiotape.

## Chapter 3: Worshiping God the Right Way

1. Michael Wiebe, "Quiet Time and the Sunday Service," *HIS Magazine,* June 1979, 13.
2. Harold S. Kushner, *When Bad Things Happen to Good People* (New York: Schocken, 1981).
3. Gary Gerew, "New Life at the Call of Faith," *Herald Journal,* 18 February 1986, A1, A5.
4. A tour guide at the Crystal Cathedral told the author that it was appropriate for Dr. Schuller to appeal to his television audience for the funds to build a facility because each seat in the cathedral would become a "revenue-producing seat" for Dr. Schuller's worldwide ministry.
5. Quoted in David Gates, "The Super Churches of Houston," *Newsweek,* 24 October 1983, 117. One church costs more than the Astrodome.
6. I am deeply indebted to Dr. Bruce Leafblad of Southwestern Baptist Seminary in Fort Worth for far more than this definition of worship. In a doctoral seminar on worship, Bruce revolutionized my thinking about worship and, as a result, my life.
7. Wayne Grundem, "Prophecy Yes, Teaching No," *Journal of the Evangelical Theological Society* (March 1987): 11–23.

## Chapter 4: The Proper Basis for Worship

1. Dietrich Bonhoeffer, *The Cost of Discipleship* (New York: Macmillan, 1959), 45.
2. Ibid., 46.
3. Ibid., 47.
4. R. C. Sproul, "The Polarization of Truth: The New Sophism," *Tabletalk,* March 1992. The entire issue addresses the matter of politically correct (PC) speech.
5. Marc Lacey, "Comments by Pastor Spark Furor," *Los Angeles Times,* 2 February 1992, B–1, B–6.
6. "Hey, I'm Terrific," *Newsweek,* 17 February 1992, 46.

## Chapter 5: The Enemies of Grace

1. Ben Patterson, "Worship Is Forever," *Christianity Today,* 1 February 1985, 15.
2. Francis A. Schaeffer, *The Great Evangelical Disaster* (Westchester, Ill.: Crossway, 1984).
3. Erwin Lutzer, "Religion a la Carte," *Moody* (July/August 1984): 65.

4. Charles W. Colson, *Loving God* (Grand Rapids: Zondervan, 1983), 12–15.

5. Kathleen Neumeyer, "God for Sale," *Los Angeles Magazine,* February 1989, 174.

6. Kenneth L. Woodward, "Pick-and-Choose Christianity," *Newsweek,* September 1984.

7. Ibid.

8. Earl Gottchalk, "A Gospel to Cheer the Me Generation," *Wall Street Journal,* 23 August 1984, 1, 14.

9. See Romans 1:22. The German philosopher Ludwig Feuerbach and others have suggested that God is made in the image of man, a mere projection of man.

10. The plate moves about four centimeters a year. Question Box, *USA Today,* 5 February 1992, B–2.

## Chapter 6: Alternatives to Grace

1. John Garraty and Peter Gay, eds., *The Columbia History of the World* (New York: Harper and Row, 1972): 957–58.

2. In *The Atheist Syndrome* (Brentwood, Tenn.: Wolgemuth and Hyatt, 1989), John P. Koster argues that Darwin, Freud, Thomas Huxley, Friedrich Nietzsche, Robert Ingersoll, and others who have greatly shaped contemporary thought were men who had deep spiritual problems: "These were men whose early childhood was marked by some form of spiritual training. They were men whose dominating, overbearing—even abusive— fathers drove them to rebellion and profound renunciation of the existence of God."

3. David Allen Hubbard, lecture presented to the Phoenix Ministerial Association, October 1968.

## Chapter 7: A Prescription for Grace

1. Charles R. Swindoll, *The Grace Awakening* (Dallas: Word, 1990), xv.

2. Robert Wenz, "The Comparative Effects of a Program of Relational Skills and Cognitive Skills upon Selected Adult Lay Persons in Witness Training Program in a Local Church Setting," D. Min. dissertation, Bethel Theological Seminary, 1990, 109–14.

3. Swindoll, *Grace Awakening,* xv.

4. "So also, when we were children, we were in slavery under the basic principles of the world" (Gal. 4:3). "See to it that no one takes you cap-

tive through hollow and deceptive philosophy, which depends on human tradition and the basic principles of this world rather than on Christ" (Col. 2:8). "Since you died with Christ to the basic principles of this world, why, as though you still belonged to it, do you submit to its rules" (Col. 2:20).

5. Jeffrey VanVonderen, *Tired of Trying to Measure Up* (Minneapolis: Bethany House, 1989), 42.

6. This model is adapted from Frank Lake, *Clinical Psychology*, abridged by Martin Yeomans (New York: Crossroads, 1987).

## Chapter 8: The Role of Worship in the Church

1. See Walter C. Kaiser, Jr., "Israel's Missionary Call," in *Perspective on the World Christian Movement*, ed. Steve Hawthorne and Ralph Winter (Pasadena, Calif.: William Carey Library, 1981), 25–33.

2. The five records of the Great Commission each express a different aspect: the strategy (Matt. 28:19); the scope (Mark 16:15); the substance (Luke 24:46–47); the sponsor (John 20:21–22); the source (Acts 1:8).

3. Gerrit Gustafson, "Worship Evangelism," *Charisma and Christian Life*, October 1991, 46–50.

4. John R. W. Stott, *Our Guilty Silence* (Downers Grove, Ill.: Inter-Varsity, 1962).

## Chapter 9: The Focus of the Worship Service

1. Paul Westermeyer, "Beyond 'Alternative' and 'Traditional' Worship," *The Christian Century*, 18 May 1992, 300–302.

2. David Fisher, "Reformation Needed for Worship," *Evangelical Action*, November/December 1986, 6.

3. Donald Macleod, *Word and Sacrament: A Preface to Preaching and Worship* (Englewood Cliffs, N.J.: Prentice-Hall, 1960): 13.

4. Robert W. Bailey, *New Ways in Christian Worship* (Nashville: Broadman, 1981), 13.

5. H. L. Willmington, *Willmington's Book of Bible Lists* (Wheaton: Tyndale House, 1987).

6. Kathleen Neumeyer, "God for Sale," *Los Angeles Magazine*, February 1989.

7. Richard Higgins, "American Interest in Religion Shallow," *The Orange County Register*, 22 April 1991, A–8.

## Chapter 10: The High Cost of Worship

1. Dennis F. Kinlaw, *Preaching in the Spirit* (Grand Rapids: Francis Asbury Press, 1985).

## Chapter 11: Renewing Our Worship

1. Editorial, *Wittenburg Door*, April/May 1978, 1–2.
2. Richard Roberts, *Revival!* (Wheaton: Tyndale House, 1978), 16.
3. Rodney Clapp, "Give Me That Old-Time Pragmatism," *Wall Street Journal*, 1 May 1987.
4. Hudson Taylor Amerding, *Leadership* (Wheaton: Tyndale House, 1978), 11.
5. The average American went from 26.2 hours of leisure time in 1973 to 16.6 hours in 1987 ("To verify . . . ," *Leadership* [Winter 1988]: 81).
6. Gustaf Neibuhr, "Churchgoers Are Putting Smaller Portion of Their Incomes into Collection Plates," *Wall Street Journal*, 31 July 1992, B–1, B–4.
7. James F. Engel, "The Road to Conversion: The Latest Research Insights," *Evangelical Missions Quarterly* (April 1990).
8. See the sharp analysis by Robert Johnson in "Heavenly Gifts: Preaching a Gospel of Acquisitiveness, a Showy Sect Prospers," *Wall Street Journal*, 11 December 1990, A–1, A–8.
9. See Joseph Bayly, "A Taste for Things Anglo," *Eternity*, December 1982, 44; and Thomas Howard, *Evangelical Is Not Enough* (Nashville: Nelson, 1984).
10. Richard Higgins, "Americans' Interest in Religion Is Shallow," *The Orange County Register*, 22 April 1991, A–8.
11. Rick Warren, "Building a Purpose-Driven Church," *The Pastor's Update* (Pasadena, Calif.: Fuller Evangelistic Association, May 1992), audiotape.
12. Robert H. Schuller, *Self-Esteem, the New Reformation* (Waco: Word, 1982), 98.
13. Quoted in Johnson, "Heavenly Gifts," A–1.
14. J. S. Whale, *Christian Doctrine* (Cambridge: Cambridge University Press, 1941), 152.
15. David McKenna, "Recovering a Sense of Awe," *United Evangelical Action*, November/December 1986, 11.
16. Chuck Swindoll, "The Fellowship of the Corner Tavern," *Leadership Journal* (Winter 1983): 27.

545233